The Rise
And Fall
Of The
BABYLONIAN
CHURCH
In
America

PAULA MATTHEWS

ṢP
Spirit & Life
Publications^{SM}

The Rise And Fall Of The Babylonian Church In America

Copyright ©2015 Paula Matthews

Cover: Paula Matthews
Back Cover: *"The Mysterious Cloud"* Photograph, courtesy of Apostle David Scott, Indianapolis

All rights reserved. No part of this book may be reproduced in any form by any electronic or mechanical means including photocopying, recording, or information storage and retrieval without permission in writing from the author.

Unless otherwise noted, scripture quotations are from
The Holy Bible: Authorized King James Version,
©2003 Thomas Nelson, Inc.

Published by
Spirit & Life Publications℠
Atlanta

Printed in the United States

Paperback ISBN: 978-0-9963218-0-8
ePub ISBN: 978-0-9963218-1-5

CONTENTS

PREFACE
Who Is He That Gave Me This Authority?   9

INTRODUCTION
God's Prophetic Word About The Babylonian Church   15
God's Original Plan For Man On Earth   19

THE RISE OF BABYLON IN THE CHURCH
The Babylonian Rebellion Against God's Plan   33
The Unholy Trinity: Religion, Tradition,   55
Commandments of Men   55
The Hidden Gospel Of The Kingdom   73

BABYLON HAS FALLEN!
Religious Pride And Deception   91
The American Dream Turned Nightmare   101
The Wine Of The Wrath Of Fornication   117
The Deceitfulness Of Riches   133

CONCLUSION
It's All About The Human Heart   151
Kingdoms May Fail, But God's Word Shall Prevail   155

ABOUT THE AUTHOR

BIBLIOGRAPHY

PREFACE

Who Is He That Gave Me This Authority?

As author of this book, I can hear the religious establishment gathering together against me saying, *"Tell us, by what authority doest thou these things? Or who is he that gave thee this authority (Luke 20:2 KJV)?"* The chief priests, scribes and elders asked Jesus this question while he was teaching the people, and preaching the gospel in the temple. He answered their question with another question, *"The baptism of John, was it from heaven, or of men?"*

These were religious men who interrupted Jesus' teaching to embarrass him before the people. When he questioned them in return, they wanted to save face in the sight of men. The people knew that these evil leaders had witnessed the multitudes who flocked to John's baptism and repented of their sins. They were also present when John announced, *"I indeed baptize you with water; but one mightier than I cometh, the latchet of whose shoes I am not worthy to unloose: he shall baptise you with the Holy Ghost and with fire: Whose fan is in his hand, and he will throughly purge his floor, and will gather the wheat into his garner; but the chaff he will burn with fire unquenchable* (Luke 3:15-17).*"* John baptized Jesus in the sight of all the people. They were there when his identity was confirmed by heaven, *"The heaven was opened, and the Holy Ghost descended in a bodily shape like a dove upon him, and a voice came from heaven, which said, Thou art my beloved Son; in thee I am well pleased* (Luke 3:21-22).*"*

The people knew that John's baptism was from heaven. What words had any other man spoken before John that would have caused all the people to repent and be baptized? Jesus said that there was no prophet greater than John (Luke 7:28), and yet the religious men rejected the word of God which he spoke. Jesus confronted them openly in the temple, and they still refused to acknowledge the truth. They knew who John was and who sent him. They also knew that Jesus had been sent by God. That is why the people were in the temple listening to him teach. These evil rulers also heard Jesus' teachings, and witnessed the signs from heaven. So He asked them (concerning John's baptism directly, and Jesus' work implied), *"Was it of heaven or of men?"* In an effort to keep from incriminating themselves in front of the people, the religious men said they could not tell where it came from. Jesus said, *"Neither tell I you by what authority I do these things (Luke 20:5-8)."* The discussion did not end there, but it bears mentioning, that no matter what truth is presented by men and women whom God sends, there will always be religious leaders who will say and do whatever is necessary to protect their reputations before the people. They consider themselves men of authority in the church. To openly confront them with the truth will often offend them. Nevertheless, God always sent his emissaries (the prophets and apostles) to openly confront leaders of the church for the sake of His flock. I am such an emissary. So, what qualifies me? God called me.

Beloved, I have been sent by God, to confront the leaders of His people. I have been sent to some of the most influential leaders of this nation, in the church, in business, in government and even in the White House. Never would I have guessed that this would have been the plan of God for my life when I received Jesus Christ as my Lord and Savior over fifty years ago. My family had been in ministry for two-three generations before my conversion. There was never a question in my mind about serving my Lord. I was called as a prophet to the nations while in my mother's womb. People recall me prophesying as early as two years old. My first face-to-face confrontation with Satan was at the age of five. I had just gotten baptized in the Baptist church, and that devil had the nerve to show up in my bedroom later that evening saying, *"Now that you are baptized, you think you're going to obey God, but you are a little kid. You have to obey your parents, and I tell **them** what to do."* I sat straight up in my bed and yelled, "You don't scare me devil!" He immediately disappeared. Looking back on that night, I realize that God had set me on a collision course with the devil that would mark my entire life and career.

I had to learn how to navigate around wicked leaders in order to obey God. I love my parents, but like most Christians, they went to church, but back then, the church was not in them. They have grown over the years as they've watched God move miraculous in my life, but in those early years, we had hell on earth. I would speak what the Lord put in my heart to speak and it nearly cost me my life as a child. My dad recalls trying to kill me. He said that it was the spirit in me that he didn't like. Later he learned that he was striving with the Spirit of God working in me. I praise God that the Holy Ghost had grown him up to understand such a thing, but for my entire life, it seemed that I was always in some sort of confrontation. People thought it was me, but it was the God in me speaking truth that no one wanted to hear. I was apparently seeing and hearing what no one else was seeing and hearing. God's voice was very clear to me, but I saw the demons working through people. The demons knew that I could see them, but the people never had a clue. For whatever reason, the Lord never explained this warfare to me until many years later when He ordained me for full-time ministry.

My spiritual training came directly from God. No man taught me how to navigate the spiritual battleground of this Babylonian world system. The Lord gifted me in the arts and sciences at a very early age. Most of my career would be spent working in television and film. I did not choose my career, God did. He told me that Hollywood was my mission field. I saw the principalities and powers of darkness at work, first hand. It was the Holy Spirit who led me every step of the way. I had an skyrocketing career, but a very rocky marriage. God was directing my career choice, but not my choice in marriage. I married the one whom God warned me to stay away from. I was very young and obedient to my parents. They wanted me to marry him, and I did. I repented to God on my wedding day, but it did not spare me from the suffering I would endure. The more God moved in my life and career, the more it shook up my marriage. This man was violent. I saw the demons in his eyes. My son was a year and a half years old, and I had enough. This man vowed that he would be the only god that I would ever serve. To back up that threat, he forbid me to pray nor to have a Bible in the house. I took it as my punishment for marrying this man against God's wishes. Then the violence escalated and death was in my face. I cried out to God and He told me that it was time to go. He said that the man had made up his mind to serve Satan in witchcraft, and there was nothing I could do. It took me three years and six attorneys to get through divorce court in the State of Illinois. During the proceedings, I learned that the man I married was connected to a mafia family. He told the mafia that I knew something that I did not know. They put a contract out on my life. Then the Lord showed it to a pastor who got together an army or prayer warriors who to this day still talk about how their prayers saved my life.

I can honestly say, that I learned obedience to God, by what I suffered. The Spirit of God was moving mightily at work in me, and at the same time, the devil was relentlessly trying to hurt me. My son was kidnapped. The satanist wanted to sacrifice my son. The people watching my son witnessed sexual behavior on his part and the authorities were contacted. An evil judge threatened me to keep my mouth shut about my son's abuse. He wrote wicked and illegal court decisions against me. When attorneys steppe up to appeal my case, they and their families were threatened. People were urging me to give up the fight, but God was directly my steps. It was causing a ripple effect throughout the courts in both Lake and Cook Counties. The Lord had already told me that if I wanted to spare my life and that of my son, I had to obey Him.

All if this evil was happening to me at the same time, and yet the Lord would not let my foot slip. He knew what I would suffer before I married that man. The devil had a plan for my life that looked like it was working, but the Lord made it clear that He was in charge, even while danger was on my every side. When I cried out to the Lord and asked why I had to deal with such evil circumstances, he said something that utterly stunned me. He said, *"It was part of His plan that I be exposed to danger and organized crime in my personal life. He said that it prepared me to deal with the real criminals: the men and women pretending to be God's leaders. The Lord said they were intentionally killing the people of God for gain. He said that their tactics were similar to those of organized crime. They did not love God or the people of God; instead, their hearts were inclined to extort them. Lord said that He was sending me head-to-head with these evil leaders, in order to take them down. They take people's money and lead them away from God. When the people are hurt or dying, these leaders cut them further with religion and eagerly watch them die. When the Lord asked me if I was ready, I told Him to lead me and I would obey His every command."*[1] The Lord spoke those words to me in 1996. In the fall of 1997, he sent me to Los Angeles to begin this new assignment.

Shortly after arriving in LA. I was filled with the Holy Spirit. God began picking me up by the spirit, taking me to different cities and countries. I would take flight every night as soon as I lay my head on my pillow. I would be preaching and teaching and laying hands on people all night long and return to my bed exhausted. One of my regular trips was to Heaven, where I would sit in with the apostles and listen to events that would happen on the earth. There was even a library, where I could open

---

[1] Matthews, Paula. "Year 2000: Move To Ohio, Journal Entries 3/00." *The War Journal (1999-2010) Volume I*. Los Angeles: Spirit & Life Publications, 2010. 121-122. Print.

a variety of books and learn of things to come. What I have learned about God's Kingdom, and the spirit realm, no man taught me. Heaven taught me all that I know. In an open vision, I found myself standing alongside the Lord, in what he called **"His Church."**[2] It was a supernatural building without walls. The place was almost empty except for the 200-300 individuals who were standing before us. This was the Lord's army, and we were inspecting the troops; his end-time leaders who were totally yielded to Him. They operated in all of the gifts as the Spirit willed. These were the ones called to do the greater works that Jesus spoke about (John 14:12). The Lord said that he was commissioning me to teach them what they needed to know in order to fulfill their assignments. Everything the Lord taught me on my visits to Heaven, I was to share with these leaders.

The Lord said that he was sending me out just like he did the first apostles to find these leaders. Many of them were in need of healing and deliverance from those who had persecuted them. This was the type of head-to-head confrontation for which the Lord had prepared me. It's as though I had walked through the darkest and most evil places on earth. I've even been to hell on a couple of occasions where the Lord taught me how to unmask the false prophets and the underworld of deception. More than once the Lord showed me in the spirit and walking through the lowest parts of hell rescuing His leaders from the pit, while dodging the bullets of the evil leaders who want to keep them there. This is the Babylonian Church experience in America.

I've gone up against spiritual leaders who were pious and religious on the outside, with hearts as black as coal and venom running through their veins on the inside. They send out their spies, hoping to find out some evil secret about your life. Others surveil your home, tap your phones and peer through your bedroom windows hoping to catch you in some illicit act. The crafty will even send prostitutes to your home, pay a woman to take off her clothes in your office, and then have an accomplice with camera in hand ready to collect evidence. Are you astounded? Don't be. Remember the woman who was accused of adultery during Jesus' day? The church leaders said she had been caught in the act and they wanted Jesus to stone her (John 8:1-11). How did they catch her in the act? They had to be watching. Where was the man? According to their law both the man and the woman should have been presented to

2   Matthews, Paula. "My Commission." *The War Journal (1999-2010) Volume I*. Los Angeles: Spirit & Life Publications, 2010. 1. Print.

be stoned. Any of them could have been the man, but it is more likely that they were using some weak soul. There had to be a man whom they could manipulate to do their dirty work, while keeping their hands clean. What evil men tried to do to me was even worse. They actually sold me as part of an online prostitution ring. The Lord alerted me that there were twelve men who intentionally wanted to destroy my life. They set me up to be killed. Men showed up demanding services that they had paid for. One man even showed up at my job. The police had suspected that someone was watching me and they put investigators on my case. The Lord had me file a case in Federal Court in what looked like an even bigger web of evil than before. The men of God set me up and now God was going to settle the score. It's happening even as I speak. This is what it is like going up against Babylon, *"the habitation of devils and the hold of every foul spirit, and a cage of every unclean and hateful bird (Revelation 18:3)."* Most of the world is under Babylon's spell, and they don't even know it. My job is to speak the truth and unchain those who want to go free. The others, well, if they don't turn, they will burn. I do what God commands and leave the rest to him.

Now that I have told you under whose authority I speak these things, let me share with you why I willingly obey my Lord. People in the church are perishing because the leaders are out of order. If there is a inkling of a chance that these leaders will turn back to God, I will do whatever the Lord commands. I will say whatever he tells me to say, for this is the mercy and grace of our Lord. It's an ugly job, but it is worth every battle with the devil, if just one soul is freed, and in position to obey God.

Beloved, God is looking for a remnant of leaders, willing to follow the plan of God for their lives. I saw the 200-300 leaders in the Lord's church. There is room for many more to join in the ranks of this powerful army. In this book, I will delve into some of the issues that led to the Babylonian rebellion of the church. I will also reveal God's glorious plan for the restoration of the church. It is a Kingdom revelation on a grand scale! There has never been anything like it on the face of this earth, nor will there ever be, until Jesus returns. This shall be the greatest finale before the return of our Lord Jesus Christ! I am honored that God chose me to be a key part of the Restoration of His Kingdom Dynasty on earth!

INTRODUCTION

God's Prophetic Word About The Babylonian Church

The Lord gave me a specific prophecy about what is going on in the American church. The rebellion of the church was about to usher in many troubles times ahead for our nation. I first wrote about these events in *The War Journal (1999-2010) Volumes I & II*. While writing those books, the Lord told me that I would get confirmation of my prophecy from another prophet of God, Dr. Oral Roberts. The Lord gave me no details of prophetic events prior to the tragedies of September 11, 2001. He made it clear, that even more tragic events would follow thereafter. Regardless of what is coming, the Lord said it was all about getting the church back into its original purpose.

In September of 2004, I got the confirmation the Lord spoke about, when Dr. Roberts publicized his prophecy entitled, **"The Wake-Up Call."** In that prophecy he stated the condition of the Church in America, according to the Lord. *"There is a wasting of My power, there is a failure to grasp the end time. And the Church, they are coming to church on Sunday, mostly for themselves. And the preachers, for the most part, are not really concerned about the nations of the earth . . . The thing that is breaking My heart is that I commanded My people, I commanded My Church to preach the gospel to the whole world and to teach all nations. And while there are evangelists and pastors and prophets and apostles and all kinds of My workers in various parts of the world and in some of the nations of the earth, it's just a drop in the bucket to what I commanded My disciples to do. And I love people so much that I cannot afford to let people go on like they are."*[1] This is indeed a wake-up call for those of use who are doing kingdom business. As this prophecy states, we have not done what all God has required. How could this be? Let me share the prophecy the Lord gave me in 2010, about the *Babylonian Church In America*. *"The Word of the Lord came to me saying: THIS IS THE AMERICAN CHURCH. And then I saw a beautifully formed, powerful physical structure in the form of a man. Atop the body was a handsome strong head; but what I saw next startled me. As the body moved, it did so without the head. There were no lacerations, no broken skin fragments about the neck. It was*

---

1   Copeland, Kenneth. "Part I, Believer's Voice Of Victory Broadcast September 27-30, 2004." *The Wake-Up Call*. Forth Worth: Kenneth Copeland Publications, 2004. 9,10,12. Print.

then that I realized; The Body and the Head were never connected! The Lord said that the Body of Christ in America was in agreement with its members. The Church was built in the similitude of the Tower of Babel."[2]

To this day, I recall my initial reaction to this vision. When I saw the Body, I was impressed with how muscular and powerful it looked; but when it walked away from the Head, I was in shock! How could we Americans attend church for all these years, and not know that it was not connected to the headship of Jesus Christ? How could we be so spiritually blind? Then the Spirit of God corrected me. The church was not blindly established. Men of God decided to pick and choose which parts of the Bible to follow. The rest of it they made up. Christian denominations were a result of men choosing what they wanted to believe about the Bible. Some believe only in the Old Testament. Others believe the New Testament. Some believe in the full gospel of the Bible. Others believe in everything except for the supernatural parts of the Bible. Jesus said, *Think not that I am come to destroy the law, or the prophets; I am not come to destroy, but to fulfil. For verily I say unto you, Till heaven and earth pass, one jot or one tittle shall in no wise pass from the law, till all be fulfilled (*Matthew 5:17-18).*"* It doesn't matter what we believe, if God has spoken it, that word will surely come to pass.

America has often been compared to ancient Babylon in her merchandising and leading people into fornication (Revelation 18). In 2001, when the twin towers were destroyed in New York, many people thought that it was a sign that Babylon had fallen. Even so, Babylon is more than a city or its buildings, Babylon is a spirit; a perverse spirit that has been working in man after Adam fell in the Garden of Eden. The spirit of Babylon is the rebellious spirit of man that makes him shun his Creator to become his own god. The spirit of Babylon convinces men that they can have the promises of God without adhering to the commands of God. The spirit of Babylon rules America and the nations of the world. People go after the American Dream because they want the Blessing of God, without God in their lives? That is not possible. The American Dream is fleeting dream for most people in the nation because they have eliminated the God factor. What happened to the nation that had once been blessed by God? How did America become known as the "new"

---

[2] Matthews, Paula."A Kingdom Divided." *The War Journal (1999-2010) Volume II*. Los Angeles: Spirit & Life Publications, 2011. 37. Print.

Babylon? In one statement: we turned from the God who Blessed us from the start. We took him out of our schools and removed him from the public square. We boldly persecute those who openly pray in his name. We create laws that offend God and place our people in bondage to sin. In her ignorance, America has cut off the Blessing and has established a new foundation in the curse.

Preachers complain about the Babylonian system of America, but God does not blame the world for the proliferation of this curse. He blames the church! The spiritual condition of the church always determines the spiritual condition of the world around us. God gave his people the authority and told us to take dominion. The church attempted to take dominion based upon religion, tradition, and the commandments of men, to no avail. Jesus said that His Church would be built upon the rock of His revelation, and that the gates of hell would not prevail against it (Matthew 16:18). The church in America rejected the rock and decided to do their own thing. Therefore they find themselves powerless against this fallen world. America could not have strayed from God, if the church had been doing her Kingdom duty in the power of His might. *"Not by might, nor by power, but by my spirit, saith the LORD of hosts (Zechariah 4:6)."*

How has the church been able to get away with such rebellion? Just like those who built the Tower of Babel, the American church had the power of agreement. The people were as one, therefore nothing was impossible for them to achieve (Genesis 11:6). The church exercised its religious power and attempted to take dominion based upon it's power of agreement amongst its members. They achieved what they desired, but the church fell short of what God commanded. Instead of being the head (Deuteronomy 28:13), the church became the tail of America; and what a ride we have had throughout the decades. The ride is now over. The Lord said that he will scatter the American Church in the imagination of their hearts. The Kingdom of God is taking over the kingdoms of this earth (including the kingdom of religion). Judgment is coming first to the church and then to the nation. The prophetic message of this book is designed to provide a detour away from death and destruction, back onto *the straight and narrow way* (Matthew 7:14). We are also determined to set the record straight concerning both the origins, and the modern-day influence of Babylon Church on the world order.

In this book, we will show how the spirit of Babylon could have never persisted in this world without the full participation of the church. The American Christian Church is ordained to take the gospel to the world. What we do and teach, others will follow. According to the Spirit of God, the nations have rebelled because the church is in rebellion. The Lord will no longer strive with the likes of religious men. Jesus is returning soon, and there is much to be done. God has to remove those who refuse to obey, and raise up another generation of leaders who will carry out His will.

Revelation (18:1-9) says that Babylon is falling and it is followed by a command from God: *"Come out of her my people!"* God does not command the world to leave Babylon. He commands the church to repent and get out of Babylon before he destroys them! God is speaking the same word to the American Church today, **"Repent and come out of Babylon or perish!"** Time is of the essence.

"But thou shalt remember the Lord thy God: for it is he that giveth thee power to get wealth, that he may establish his covenant which he sware unto they father as it is this day. And it shall be, if thou do at all forget the Lord thy God, and walk after other gods, and serve them, and worship them, I testify against you this day that ye shall surely perish. As the nations which the Lord destroyeth before your face, so shall ye perish; because ye would not be obedient unto the voice of the Lord your God."
(Deuteronomy 8:18-20)

God's Original Plan For Man On Earth

To understand how the Babylonian spirit began, we must go back to God's original plan for man on earth. According to the Bible, we know that in the beginning, God created the heavens and the earth. The Bible also tells us that God was pleased with the work of his hands and God saw that, *"it was very good* (Genesis 1:31).*"* Genesis Chapter 1 repeatedly tells us that everything God created was very good. Things today are not so good. In fact, it seems that quite the opposite is true. What happened to God's creation? How could all of creation go from very good to very bad in our limited human existence? What cataclysmic event could have occurred to cause such a significant moral and physical decline? When did such an event happen in human history? Who was responsible? In this chapter we will explore all of these questions by taking a journey back to creation and a brief look at the history of mankind.

The Bible tells us that God made all of creation in six days. When he created man on that sixth day, God created his masterpiece; a human in the likeness and image of God himself (Genesis 1:26-27). *"And the LORD God formed man of the dust of the ground, and breathed into his nostrils the breath of life; and man became a living soul (Genesis 2:7)."* Finally, God had what he had always longed for; a family. It began with his first born son, whom He named Adam (mankind). God pronounced a Blessing upon mankind (Adam) saying, *"Be fruitful, and multiply, and replenish the earth, and subdue it: and have dominion over the fish of the sea, and over the fowl of the air, and over every living thing that moveth upon the earth* (Genesis 1:28).*"* Everything God created prior to Adam, was created for the pleasure of God's family on earth. This was the desire of God for mankind (Revelation 4:11).

God created a garden called Eden (pleasure), and there he placed Adam (mankind). There were only good things in Eden, all for the pleasure of mankind. There was no sickness or death; only good things that were pleasing to the eyes and good to eat. The garden was watered by a river that parted into four major rivers that led to more lands filled with gold and precious gems in that garden (Genesis 2:10-14). Adam was created to be the first of many brethren in the family of God. He was charged with replicating what God had done in the garden and spreading it across the earth, and replenishing whatever was lacking in creation for all eternity. This was an enormous task for Adam and God determined that he needed help in fulfilling his destiny. So, he created woman. *"And the LORD God caused a deep sleep to fall upon Adam, and he slept: and he took one of his ribs, and closed up the flesh instead thereof; And the rib, which the LORD God had taken from man, made he a woman, and brought her unto the man. And Adam said, This is now bone of my bones, and flesh of my flesh: she shall be called Woman, because she was taken out of Man. Therefore shall a man leave his father and his mother, and shall cleave unto his wife: and they shall be one flesh. And they were both naked, the man and his wife, and were not ashamed. And Adam called his wife's name Eve; because she was the mother of all living* (Genesis 2:21-25; 3:20).*"*

So far, I have just restated the story of creation from the stand point of what God designed for his human creation. This is the heart and mind of God towards his human creation. It still remains today. God never changed his mind about providing only good for mankind. That was his original plan and it continues to be God's plan today (Jeremiah 29:11). He only created good things for his family, it was never suppose to decrease. It was to increase and multiply throughout the whole earth. God created only the best for his son. Earth was supposed to be the inheritance for Adam and Eve and all of their descendants, for all eternity. This was *eternal life*. Where they would live forever with God their Father; His love and goodness pouring down from heaven. These were designed to be days of heaven upon the earth, for all mankind. God had trained Adam to rule on earth as his Father ruled in heaven. God gave him the earth and gave him dominion. God also gave Adam seed. As long as there is seed, mankind could produce whatever God designed for this earth. In fact, everything God created had within itself the necessary seed to reproduce itself (Genesis 1:11-12). This would ensure that creation would remain fruitful and *replenish* itself over time. When we think of replenish, we think of something running out, that is not what this word *replenish* means. God intended for everything in earth to be in abundance, always full, even overflowing. His promises today are still for abundance. The Prophet David captured this idea of abundance in the Psalm 23. *"Thou preparest a table before me in the presence of mine enemies: thou anointest my head with oil; my cup runneth over* (Psalm 23:5).*"* The Prophet Jeremiah spoke these words to the Babylonian captives of his day, *"For I know the thoughts that I think toward you, saith the LORD, thoughts of peace, and not of evil, to give you an expected end (Jeremiah 29:11)."* Even though they were in captivity, God wanted his people to know that this was never his plan for their lives. His plan was always for their peace *(Shalom)* which includes welfare, wealth, health, and prosperity.

This plan for mankind's peace was echoed throughout the prophets and the New Testament. It was, and continues to be God's desire to Bless and multiply his people in every good thing. Jesus said that he came to give us life and that more abundantly (John 10:10). It may seem impossible for such abundance to happen in our day, but with God, all things are possible. Today, it is the job of the Holy Spirit to lead us to that place of abundance, where God is able to do *"exceeding abundantly above all that we ask or think, according to the power that worketh in us* (Ephesians 3:20)." It is the grace of God, the divine life and purpose of God that flows out of heaven onto the lives of men on earth. God's grace is his favor and good will, but it comes from a wellspring out of heaven. This grace does not come because we are so perfect. It is shed upon us because of God's covenant with the earth. Grace provides what we need to do God's will in the earth. *"And God is able to make all grace abound toward you; that ye, always having all sufficiency in all things, may abound to every good work* (II Corinthians 9:8)." Grace is supplied through the spirit. It supernaturally empowers us to come into that wealthy place God originally designed for man. Grace is a powerful thing in that has the ability to eradicate our past and catapult us into our God given destiny. Grace literally treats man as if sin never existed. It is a complete reversal of everything that Adam's curse brought upon the earth.

Only a loving Father, like God could have thought of such a magnificent plan for mankind, and yet since the sin of Adam, mankind has consistently rejected God's plan. In the next chapter we will explain why Adam sinned and how sin continues to perpetuate the case of man versus God until this day. God's original plan for man was a glorious plan; a lavish plan of wealth and prosperity that was designed to multiply and remain full throughout all eternity . . . and why not? God is an extravagant God. If you venture into the Book of Revelation, you will find that heaven is a very extravagant place, it should not be surprising that God would lavish the same on his earthly sons. *"And the building of the wall of it was of jasper: and the city was pure gold, like unto clear glass. And the foundations of the wall of the city were garnished with all manner of precious stones. The first foundation was jasper; the second, sapphire; the third, a chalcedony; the fourth, an emerald; The fifth, sardonyx; the sixth, sardius; the seventh, chrysolite; the eighth, beryl; the ninth, a topaz; the tenth, a chrysoprasus; the eleventh, a jacinth; the twelfth, an amethyst. And the twelve gates were twelve pearls; every several gate was of one pearl: and the street of the city was pure gold, as it were transparent glass* (Revelation 21:18-21)." Eden was an earthly reflection of heaven. This earthly paradise was to be the inheritance for the sons of God. This lavishness is a reflection of God himself. This was the Glory of God manifesting in the earth for the benefit of His son. This was a love feast, an offering of all that God had, to the one He loved with all of His heart. *"Behold, what manner of love the Father hath bestowed upon us, that we should be called the sons of God* (I John 3:1)." Let this saturate your mind and sink into your spirit. God loves us beyond human comprehension. That will never change. It can never change, because God **is** Love (I John 4:8). All Love could ever give, is lavish love to those whom He loves.

The Lord gave me personal revelation many years ago. One day, I was praying and I asked God to explain his purpose for the Bible. Why did Jesus really come? The answer he gave me was not an answer that you would hear in many churches today. The Lord took me through Genesis to Revelation in a vision and he simply said, **"I was looking for a family."** It struck me somewhat odd that God needed a family. I heard his words, but in my spirit I knew that God really needed a family. Then he continued. **"I needed a family in which I can give an inheritance."** What he gave me was quite simple and quite odd at the same time. God had a need. It never occurred to me that God would have a need. After all, this is God! He is all knowing (omniscient). He is ever present (omnipresent). He is Almighty God (omnipotent). How could he have a need? And yet, there was an air of desperation in his voice as he said, **"I needed a family in which I could give an inheritance."** The inheritance that he spoke of was not only in heaven, but it was available on earth. Years later, the Lord would show me that this inheritance was called ***"Eden."*** This was the same Eden that Adam and Eve knew in that garden. It never left the earth, it was just hidden for the sons of God today.

I am giving the prophetic vision for God's Kingdom plan for man on earth. I am deliberately avoiding the discussion of Adam's sin and how he was exiled from Eden. We will discuss that later. My focus is on God's original plan for mankind. The American Church focuses so much on sin, that they never get to the inheritance. This is not how God does it. He tells you who you are In Him. Then, he shows you the inheritance. He is disappointed that men choose sin over goodness. God desperately seeks to express his goodness in the earth. In the mind of God, the only reason sin was mentioned was because it disqualified mankind from receiving the inheritance. Sin also cuts us off from the eternal life that God originally deigned. Man was never created to die. He was supposed to live with God forever. That was the original plan. When sin entered into the picture, it had to be dealt with so that mankind could once again qualify for his Godly inheritance. That is why Jesus came to earth. To restore the inheritance to mankind. It was always about our heavenly Father wanting to Bless his sons in the earth.

In the minds of most Christians, God is not Father. He is a domineering ruler somewhere in the heavens. When Jesus came to earth talking about God being his Father, the Jews of his day were outraged. How dare Jesus say he is the son of God! The ancient Jews were steeped in religious rituals and doctrines of men. They honored God with their lips, but their hearts were far from him. They could not relate to God as a father; a lawgiver, yes, but God was never their Father. They referred to themselves as sons of Abraham, but never sons of God. In their eyes, that was blasphemous. For Jesus to claim himself as son of God, that also meant that he was the Messiah, their earthly ruler and king. They rejected that notion all together and thereby forfeited their inheritance. The message of Jesus Christ and his kingdom was then sent to the Gentiles (non Jewish unbelievers). It was the assignment of the church to take the message to the world. The early church was the model for all others to follow, but like the Jews, the American Church rejected Jesus as Lord and also forfeited their inheritance. So what will God do next? He is about to raise up **His Church** in the midst of us. This will be a powerful army of sons of God to ever grace this earth. They will perform the "greater works" Jesus spoke about before he left this earth. **His Church** will walk in the full power and dominion as God designed from the foundation of the world. They will also revisit Eden, walking in their inheritance and experiencing days of heaven upon this earth.

The life and ministry of Jesus reflected all that God designed for Adam. That is why the Apostle Paul called Jesus the last Adam (I Corinthians 15:45). We are the Body of Christ. When God sees us, he sees Jesus. We are sons and heirs of God; and joint heirs with Jesus (Romans 8:14-17). That means that everything that God has is shared jointly between Jesus and all of the sons of God. What does God have? Psalm 24:1 says it best, *"The earth is the LORD'S, and the fulness thereof; the world, and they that dwell therein."* This may also surprising to some of you, but Jesus died to restore to all mankind; power, riches, wisdom, strength, honor, glory and blessing (Revelation 12:5). This was part of the inheritance that God originally gave to Adam. Jesus came to restore it back to us. Remember how Jesus arose from the dead saying, *"All power is given unto me in heaven and in earth. Go ye therefore, and teach all nations, baptizing them in the name of the Father, and of the Son, and of the Holy Ghost: Teaching them to observe all things whatsoever I have commanded you: and, lo, I am with you alway, even unto the end of the world. Amen* (Matthew 28:18-20).*"* This was the same charge that God gave to Adam, *"And God blessed them, and God said unto them, Be fruitful, and multiply, and replenish the earth, and subdue it: and have dominion* (Genesis 1:28).*"* You might say, "Jesus gave them dominion, but how did he tell them to be fruitful or multiply, or subdue the earth?" I'm glad you asked. You first need to understand that when God first Blessed Adam, the world was perfect. There was no sin, sickness or death, neither was there anything lacking in the earth. By the time Jesus came along, there has been many centuries of death and devastation. The commanded Jesus gave the church was that of restoration; restoring things back to God's original plan, which would produce the same results that Adam had at creation. So, although the command of Jesus and the Blessing of God are not exactly the same in words, they produce exactly the same results in the earth.

Let's take a brief look at what Jesus taught. In the Babylonian church they teach about sin. They teach about heaven and hell, but few teach about the Kingdom. Few understand the Kingdom, yet the gospel of the Kingdom was the only message Jesus taught, even after his resurrection (Acts 1:1-3). It was the only message he commanded his disciples to teach (Mark 16:14-20). Even though we have not yet discussed the fall of Adam in the garden in detail, for now, just know that Jesus came to restore all that Adam lost. Let this suffice for now, because I want you to see the BIG picture, which is God's original plan for man on earth.

That is what the gospel represented, God's original intent for our lives. That plan has never changed. Men have strayed from the plan and chose religion, but God never changed. His original plan for us still stands. That is why Jesus came. God anointed him with the Holy Ghost and power so that he could go about doing good and healing all that were oppressed by the devil (Acts 10:38). The devil is the same serpent we saw in the garden of Eden (Revelation 12:9). Religion watered down the works of Jesus, but he came demonstrating the **dominion** of the Kingdom over every thing that creeps upon the earth (Genesis 1:28); over every demonic spirit, every evil power of darkness, even over the cunning serpent (satan aka devil) who came creeping in the garden and has been deceiving mankind ever since.

Jesus came to return us to Eden, and to the love of the Father; to the Blessing that makes us rich without sorrow (Proverbs 10:22). The thief came to steal, kill and destroy mankind (John 10:10). He has tricked us out of our dominion through our own ignorance. Jesus came to destroy the works of the devil and return to us God's abundant life (I John 3:8; John 10:10). Jesus came preaching and demonstrating the power of the gospel over sickness, disease, demons, blindness, lameness, all forms of lack and death. His greatest demonstration of kingdom power was when he resurrected from the dead, and resurrected with all power in heaven and earth in his hand. Jesus commanded us to go in that power (Matthew 28:18) and preach the gospel to every creature. The Lord promised to confirm the word preached, with signs following (Mark 16:20). Here is the most amazing part, Jesus said that whoever believed what they preached would also have signs following them. This the power of the preaching of the gospel that the American Church never realized. Jesus said, *"And these signs shall follow them that believe; In my name shall they cast out devils; they shall speak with new tongues; They shall take up serpents; and if they drink any deadly thing, it shall not hurt them; they shall lay hands on the sick, and they shall recover* (Mark 16:17-28)." Are you hearing this? Jesus said that wherever the gospel is preached, anyone who believes will walk in the same signs that Jesus and the disciples walked in. So, if we are not seeing more and more people walking in signs and wonders of the gospel that means that either the people are not receiving what they have heard, or that the preachers today are preaching something other than the gospel. So what is going on?

In a recent magazine article, I gave the prophetic word the Lord spoke concerning this issue. He said that **the people of God had gotten the idea that "signs and wonders only follow great men and women of God."**[1] Therefore, the power of the gospel is not being demonstrated in America as God desires. Some leaders are demonstrating the power of God, but the laymen are not catching on. They just don't believe it is possible for them. The world is desperate to see some sign that God is still doing miracles, but the people of God are not responding. They seem to be in their own *Christian bubble*, unconcerned about the world around them. Jesus commanded us to take this gospel and it's miraculous signs around the world. In general, Americans are refusing to obey. They don't realize that God has called each of us for a specific purpose. It's a purpose that establishes Kingdom dominion for a family, community, and even a nation. When we don't obey, people continue to suffer under satanic oppression; whether it is poverty, disease or human degradation. The Lord brought this to my attention a couple of years ago. I was listening to a television plea from a ministry asking for help to feed people in Africa. In my heart I asked God, "Why hasn't the famine lifted?" How could there be generations of famine in one country when missionaries are working hard to help them. The Lord said that he gave solutions to his people in America, but they refused to go.

Here is a quote from the blog post I wrote concerning this issue. **"The Spirit of God says that there is no lack of resources, only a lack of obedient people who are willing to share their time and resources with others. And, when we refuse to obey God, we curse ourselves."**[2] Our Kingdom command is to go into all the world preaching and demonstrating the power of the Kingdom which releases the Blessing that will always multiply (increase) our resources. The Blessing will always cause us to replenish what is lacking and bring it back into prosperity. That is how we subdue and take dominion over poverty, and lack in the world. This is what the early church did right after the resurrection. They obeyed the commanded to go and be a witness of the resurrection. *"But ye shall receive power, after that the Holy Ghost is come upon you: and ye shall be witnesses unto me both in Jerusalem, and in all Judaea, and in Samaria, and unto the uttermost part of the earth (Acts 1:8)."* Their witness of the resurrection was the greatest demonstration of Kingdom

---

1   Matthews, Paula. "Kingdom Duty." *Grace For Living Magazine (Digital Edition)*. Spirit & Life Publications℠, 30 Sep. 2015. Web. 20 Nov. 2015.
2   Matthews, Paula. "Our Obedience Yields Solutions To End Poverty." *Thinking Outside Of The Box*. 16 June 2012. Web. 20 Nov. 2015.

power ever seen in their day. This was proof that the Kingdom had dominion and that the curse had ended, for all who would believed. The church grew in great numbers and joy filled the cities when people saw the miracles (Acts 8:8). Poverty had ended for those who believed, to the point that no one suffered lack (Acts 4:34-35). When the apostles obeyed Jesus' command to be a witness, great grace came upon them all. Every financial need was met. There was no lack. Why was this? All those who believed *were one,* as Jesus, God and the Holy Spirit were one (John 17:21-23).They were of one heart and one soul, believing and speaking the same thing for the benefit of the Kingdom. Contrast this attitude with that of those who built the Tower of Babel. They were also one heart and one soul, but against God and his kingdom. They were in agreement to build a city whose tower would reach to heaven so that they could make a name for themselves. Just like the early church, the people in Babel were one. Here is what the Lord observed, *"And the LORD said, Behold, the people is one, and they have all one language; and this they begin to do: and now nothing will be restrained from them, which they have imagined to do (Genesis 11:6)."* The people of Babel were in agreement to rebel against the command of God. So what did the Lord do? He confused their speech so they could no longer understand each other. Then he scattered them abroad from Babel over the face of the earth (Genesis 11:7-8). The early church had joy, peace and prosperity. The people of Babel got terror and confusion. In any case, the will of the Lord was done. One saw glory and Blessing. The other saw the curse. Which was the better choice? You decide. I choose the Blessing. It's the simpler, more beneficial choice. We need only obey the Spirit of God when he says, *"Go Ye!"* This choice results in our reigning in Kingdom dominion, and demonstrates why Jesus came to earth.

The gospel that Jesus taught was about the return of power and dominion to the sons of God in the earth. Those who are in Christ have been raised to sit together with him in the heavenly places (Ephesians 2:4-10). This is our seat of power and dominion in the kingdom. In the church, people believe that Jesus has power, but few really believe that the same power has been given to us. Before the resurrection, there was no indwelling of the Holy Spirit to empower men. When Jesus sent out the seventy apostles, they were not saved either, and yet they came back saying,*"Lord, even the devils are subject unto us through thy name. And he said unto them, I beheld Satan as lightning fall from heaven. Behold, I give unto you power to tread on serpents and scorpions, and over all the power of the enemy: and nothing shall by any means hurt you* (Luke 10:17-19).*"* This was the power and dominion connection with the Christ (the anointed One and his anointing). As mere men, what the seventy did was impossible, but when they obeyed the command to go preach the gospel, all things became possible for them, even power over the devil. Jesus said that when he spoke the word, that it was the father that did the work (John 14:10). The same was true for those who followed Jesus. Notice that God was determined that man would have dominion over evil, even before the resurrection. Jesus came to raise us up in power over sickness, lack and death (the curse of Adam), and back into Blessing that Adam lost. Jesus told us to preach this gospel of God's grace that has been given to men, so they could return to Eden. Jesus gave us the Holy Spirit, the earnest deposit of our inheritance. When we speak and obey the word of God, the Holy Spirit in us brings forth an awesome display of kingdom power to overcome the evil of this world. Our demonstration of faith and power, is what overcomes the evil of this world (I John 5:4). This is our witness to the truth of why Jesus came.

Now, I know that my interpretation of the gospel is a bit different than the version that is typically preached in churches today. Most don't talk about Adam, but about Abraham, Moses and the Jews. There is nothing wrong with telling it that way because when the Bible was written it was from the Jewish perspective. The Lord told me how to teach the gospel. In a vision, he showed me the time line of human history on earth. He talked about Adam, Noah, David, Solomon, Abraham, Moses, and the prophets. He showed me Jesus. He said that *"the shortest distance between two points is a line."* The Lord then drew a line from Adam to Jesus and said that this is the most important part of the gospel message. It involved the first and the last Adam; and it includes the patriarchs of the Bible, the Jews and the church, but **all** of humanity. The gospel message was always about returning mankind to Eden and to the inheritance; to their rightful place as sons of God in the earth. Sin just happened to be in the way and had to be dealt with. Otherwise, God would have never mentioned sin, the curse <u>or</u> death. How about one more confirmation? Out of the mouth of two or three witnesses shall every word be established (II Corinthians 13:1). We gave you the witness from Genesis, and also that from Jesus' gospel of the kingdom. Let's now look at Revelation Chapter 21,when John describes his vision of the *holy city of God*. *"And I heard a great voice out of heaven saying, Behold, the tabernacle of God is with men, and he will dwell with them, and they shall be his* *people, and God himself shall be with them, and be their God. And God shall wipe away all tears from their eyes; and there shall be no more death, neither sorrow, nor crying, neither shall there be any more pain: for the former things are passed away. And he that sat upon the throne said, Behold, I make all things new. And he said unto me, Write: for these words are true and faithful. And he said unto me, It is done. I am Alpha and Omega, the beginning and the end. I will give unto him that is athirst of the fountain of the water of life freely. He that overcometh shall inherit all things; and I will be his God, and he shall be my son* (Revelation 21:1-7). " Imagine seeing a new heaven and a new earth and a heavenly city where there was no more death, nor sorrow, or crying or pain. This inheritance is only for God's sons. The Lord said that he was *making all things new*. This means returning all things to his original plan. In Christ, we become new creatures born of God (II Corinthians 5:17). You must be born again into the family of God. This passage says *he that overcomes* shall be God's son. We are overcomers by faith in Jesus Christ. Those who receive Jesus are given the right to become sons (John 1:12). Becoming born again is a supernatural process in which the Holy Spirit of God comes to reside in your heart. Then we are commanded to live by faith, and not by sight (II Corinthians 5:7) like the rest of the world. It is the Holy Spirit in us, that helps us over come the lust of this world. Roman 8:14 says that those who are led by the Spirit of God are the sons of God. The Holy Spirit is also the executor of our inheritance. He leads us to the promises of God.

Today, when men accept Jesus Christ as Lord, this enables them to return to Eden. I know about this Eden. I've been there myself. Here is my personal account of Eden[3] *"The Lord began talking to me about his glory manifesting in the lives of men on earth. He said that this glory was Eden. My spirit began crying out to God to lay hold of everything that he has for my life. I could hear it in my sleep. I wanted to lay hold of that for which Jesus laid hold of me. This had been going on for months. One day I heard the voice of the Lord say, "PAULA BE!" Then he gave me a vision that astounded me. In the vision I was carrying a heavy royal mantle along with a crown and a scepter. I laid those things down and began bathing in what seemed to be a murky pool. The vision zoomed out and I saw that the murky pool was a pool of blood at the bottom of a hill that extended from the foot of the cross where Jesus*

---

[3] Matthews, Paula."My Adventure To Eden."*Seeking And Enjoying The True Treasure Of This Life*. Shaker Heights: Spirit & Life Publications[SM], 2013. 33-34. Print.

had been crucified. I kept dunking myself in the pool when the Lord appeared. At this point in the vision and I found myself at a place in the spirit where several dimensions in time had intersected. The Lord was standing with me in the pool, and yet I looked up the hill and I could see his feet nailed to the cross and the blood was still alive and it was streaming down upon us. Then the Lord immersed me in the pool. It seemed like I was being baptized in that pool of blood at the bottom of the hill at the foot of the cross. When I came up out of the pool, the Lord began wringing out my hair. He was standing besides me and I noticed that he had to fully extend his right arm and turned to use his left hand to wring out my hair. When the Lord let my hair go, it landed at its full length in the center of my back.

The Lord placed the crown on my head and helped me put on my mantle. He placed the scepter in my right hand and he grabbed my left hand and we began walking out of the pool alongside the bottom of the hill, but behind where the cross was extended. I didn't know where we were going there were only rocks and no exits Then the Lord moved forward only a few steps from the pool of blood, and a portal appeared. I saw a golden sky, beautiful trees and meadows that seemed to appear from out of nowhere. It was then that I realized how grey and sullen the atmosphere was at the pool. This place thru the portal was beautiful! When the Lord and I stepped through the portal, our clothes had also changed. We were both wearing a white robe and a golden crown. We were holding hands, running and laughing like two little children. The Lord said, "You did it! Welcome to the Kingdom!" This was it! This was the Garden of Eden that Adam saw. "That's all I had to do?" "That was easy," I replied. The Lord said, "Now, go and tell the others and invite them to come here as well." The vision ended as I basked in the splendor of the kingdom knowing that I had bridged the gap between heaven and earth; between time and space; and I had entered into a dimension where God's purpose intersected with my desire. This was Eden."

Beloved, that was my personal account of Eden, and as it reads, the Lord has told me to tell others and invite them there as well. I found Eden when I went after everything God had for me. This was the cry of my heart. II Chronicles 16:9 says that, *"For the eyes of the LORD run to and fro throughout the whole earth, to shew himself strong in the behalf of them whose heart is perfect toward him."* God is always desperately looking for a heart that is full of faith; a heart that is ready to believe that

God is who he says he is; and that God will indeed do what he says he will do. God desires to find a willing and obedient heart; one that loves as God loves and desires what God desires for the people of the earth.

After Adam, God found Noah, Solomon, Esther, Abraham and others. All who had the heart to go after God's purpose, prevailed in this earth. God Blessed them and made their names great. These were those who feared the Lord and delighted greatly in his commandments. Their seed was mighty upon the earth (BE FRUITFUL AND MULTIPLY). Wealth and riches were in their houses (REPLENISH). These were those who were not afraid of evil tidings: their hearts were fixed, trusting in the LORD. Their hearts were established. They would not move until they saw their desire upon their enemies (SUBDUE AND HAVE DOMINION). God exalted them with dignity and honor. Their righteousness endures forever (Psalm 112:1-3,7-8, 9).

Even as I finish writing this chapter, I hear the Holy Spirit telling me that Eden was where I had experienced the Lord's Holy Hill. Now for the invitation for all to come as well:

> *"Who shall ascend into the hill of the LORD?*
> *Or who shall stand in his holy place?*
> *He that hath clean hands, and a pure heart;*
> *Who hath not lifted up his soul unto vanity, nor sworn deceitfully.*
> *He shall receive the blessing from the LORD,*
> *And righteousness from the God of his salvation.*
> *This [is] the generation of them that seek him,*
> *That seek thy face, O Jacob. Selah.*
> *Lift up your heads, O ye gates; and be ye lift up, ye everlasting doors;*
> *And the King of glory shall come in. (Psalm 24:3-7)."*

If after reading this chapter, you desire to step into God's original plan for your life, then take the first step by becoming born again into the family of God. Say the following prayer out loud,

Dear God in Heaven,
I now know and believe that you have a great inheritance for my life, that your thoughts for me are for good and not evil; to give me a future and hope that I have longed for. I am sorry that I rebelled against you by creating plans for my own life; following after the ways of ordinary men, when your plan is far greater than anything I could have imagined on my own. I want to be born again into your family, to receive your inheritance. I renounce Satan and my past and desire to step into your original plan for my life. Therefore I receive Jesus Christ as my Lord and Savior. Fill me with your Holy Spirit. Holy Spirit, lead me daily to the perfect will of God for my life. Thank you Jesus for taking back my inheritance. Thank you God, my father for loving me and providing such an inheritance for me. I will love and serve you with my whole heart, for the rest of my days on earth, and look forward to spending an eternity loving you forever more.
In Jesus' Name I Pray
Amen

THE RISE OF BABYLON IN THE CHURCH

The Babylonian Rebellion Against God's Plan

In the previous chapter we spent quite a bit of time discussing God's glorious plan for men on earth. We talked about how all throughout history God desired a family in which to give his inheritance. This inheritance would determine who would rule and reign on earth. Whoever ruled and reigned would have dominion over the earth forever. As glorious as that inheritance was, from the very beginning, there was a battle over who was the rightful heir. The battle for dominion began in heaven. The Tower of Babel became the lasting symbol of those who openly claimed an inheritance, they did not qualify to receive. This was a battle over sonship <u>and</u> dominion, which rages on even to this day.

The Babylonian mind-set began long before the Tower of Babel. This spirit is satanic in nature. It began with the luciferian rebellion in heaven. Here is the Prophet Isaiah's account of what happened, *"How art thou fallen from heaven, O Lucifer, son of the morning! [how] art thou cut down to the ground, which didst weaken the nations! For thou hast said in thine heart, I will ascend into heaven, I will exalt my throne above the stars of God: I will sit also upon the mount of the congregation, in the sides of the north: I will ascend above the heights of the clouds; I will be like the most High. Yet thou shalt be brought down to hell, to the sides of the pit* (Isaiah 14:12-15).*"* Lucifer was an angel in heaven until he rebelled against God, and was exiled to earth. You will also know him as Satan, that Old Serpent, the Devil, and the Father of Lies.

Let's hear what the Prophet Ezekiel had to say about this anointed cherub, *"Thus saith the Lord GOD; Thou sealest up the sum, full of wisdom, and perfect in beauty. Thou hast been in Eden the garden of God; every precious stone was thy covering, the sardius, topaz, and the diamond, the beryl, the onyx, and the jasper, the sapphire, the emerald, and the carbuncle, and gold: the workmanship of thy tabrets and of thy pipes was prepared in thee in the day that thou wast created. Thou art the anointed cherub that covereth; and I have set thee so: thou wast upon the holy mountain of God; thou hast walked up and down in the midst of the stones of fire. Thou wast perfect in thy ways from the day that thou wast created, till iniquity was found in thee. By the multitude of thy merchandise they have filled the midst of thee with violence, and thou hast sinned: therefore I will cast thee as profane out of the mountain of God: and I will destroy thee, O covering cherub, from the midst of the stones of fire. Thine heart was lifted up because of thy beauty, thou hast corrupted thy wisdom by reason of thy brightness: I will cast thee to the ground, I will lay thee before kings, that they may behold thee* (Ezekiel 28:12-17)." When Lucifer was cast out of heaven, he and his angels were exiled to earth. Lucifer was no longer a beautiful angel, but a slithering snake destined to crawl upon the dust of the ground. He was no longer an anointed heavenly being, but a lowly beast, destined to be ruled over by another. How was he going to exalt his throne above God's?

God exiled Lucifer and his angels to this earth for a purpose. Then God did something that astounded even the angels. He created an unknown species of being called man. *"What is man, that thou art mindful of him? Or the son of man, that thou visitest him* (Hebrews 2:6)?" From the dust of the ground, the very dust upon which the serpent was exiled to creep, God made a man in his likeness and image. To add insult to injury, God gave man dominion over every beast. Now the covering angel who wanted to exalt his throne above God was being subjected to be dominated by a man who was in every way like God. God, then placed man in the garden, knowing that the serpent was also there. Lucifer was already exiled. Was Adam to be his jailer, or was God intentionally setting up a spiritual confrontation on the earth? The serpent still wanted to be ruler over his own kingdom, but he had no power to create one for himself. The only way he could get a kingdom would be to steal one from someone else, and that was his plan for Adam. If he could just find a weakness in the man. If he could just find a way to take that weakness and make the man forfeit his power, all the kingdoms of this world would be his.

God created man, **and gave him every good thing** in the garden. God withheld no good thing from the man except the tree of the knowledge of good and evil. *"And the LORD God took the man, and put him into the garden of Eden to dress it and to keep it. And the LORD God commanded the man, saying, Of every tree of the garden thou mayest freely eat: But of the tree of the knowledge of good and evil, thou shalt not eat of it: for in the day that thou eatest thereof thou shalt surely die* (Genesis 2:15-17)." Most of you know how this story goes. The serpent talked Eve into eating from the forbidden tree and she gave the fruit to her husband and he also ate. This serpent had some serious skills of deception and manipulation (Genesis 3:1). How else could he have convinced Eve to eat the fruit while Adam stood by and watched? Why would Eve even hold a conversation with a serpent in the first place? Adam was standing with Eve and witnessed the entire conversation, why didn't he step up and defend his wife against the serpent? Why didn't they just go back to God and tell what the serpent said? What was it that captured their attention so much that is caused them not to respond in a way consistent with God's command? The serpent tempted them, yes, but it was the lust of their hearts that led them to eat from that tree. *"But every man is tempted, when he is drawn away of his own lust and enticed. Then when lust hath conceived, it bringeth forth sin: and sin, when it is finished, bringeth forth death (James 1:14-15)."*

Take a look at the conversation between Eve and the serpent. *"Yea, hath God said, Ye shall not eat of every tree of the garden? And the woman said unto the serpent, We may eat of the fruit of the trees of the garden: But of the fruit of the tree which is in the midst of the garden, God hath said, Ye shall not eat of it, neither shall ye touch it, lest ye die. And the serpent said unto the woman, Ye shall not surely die: For God doth know that in the day ye eat thereof, then your eyes shall be opened, and ye shall be as gods, knowing good and evil. And when the woman saw that the tree was good for food, and that it was pleasant to the eyes, and a tree to be desired to make one wise, she took of the fruit thereof, and did eat, and gave also unto her husband with her; and he did eat (Genesis 3:1-6)."*

This had to be the opportunity the serpent had waited for. He had to see the lust in their eyes when Eve saw that the tree was good for food. She lusted after that fruit with her eyes. Every tree in the garden was pleasant to the eyes and good for food, but the tree of knowledge of good and evil would was different. It would make them wise and make them like gods. They were already like God. He withheld no good thing from them. If they had just asked, God would have surely told them everything they needed to know, but alas, it was too late. Sin came forth when they took the fruit and ate it. The curse had been activated and the process of death had begun. Instead of multiplying the Blessing in the earth, Adam and Eve multiplied the curse, which resulted in a death sentence for every human who would ever be born on earth. Remember that it was God's plan is to find a family in which he can give an inheritance. Adam and

Eve were no longer qualified, but there were also no other humans in the earth. By default, the serpent would rule. How was that possible if God gave man dominion? The serpent was a creature, not at man. He could not create a man in his own image, nor could he turn himself into a man. His tactic to rule on earth had to evolve as mankind evolved in the curse. So what did he do? That serpent who used his subtle powers to deceive Eve in the garden, continues to deceive the whole world (Revelation 12:9) even in our day. When God cursed him it set the stage for the luciferian battle to continue, this time with mankind given the authority to exercise the power of heaven upon the earth. God said to the serpent, *"Because thou hast done this, thou art cursed above all cattle, and above every beast of the field; upon thy belly shalt thou go, and dust shalt thou eat all the days of thy life: And I will put enmity between thee and the woman, and between thy seed and her seed; it shall bruise thy head, and thou shalt bruise his heel (Genesis 3:14-15)."* This was God's declaration of the sentence that satan would serve in the earth. The seed of the woman would now be at war with the seed of the serpent. At the end of this battle, the seed of the woman would destroy him. For the power of heaven's justice to be served, Jesus Christ was that seed who destroyed satan on the cross, and made an open show of him by resurrecting from the dead (Colossians 2:114-15).

We are still talking about the Babylonian spirit, but it was necessary to see how this rebellion relates to things in heaven <u>and</u> in earth. Although men have rebelled against God throughout history, they have not acted on their own. Satan and his fallen angels have an army of demons who have been very busy deceiving men, just like the serpent did to Eve. According to the battle that God declared to the world, mankind would eventually prevail and recapture dominion over the earth. Bible history has taught us that without the Spirit of God operating in their lives, ordinary men are not capable of winning the battle against Satan and his armies. Many would fall prey to his tactics. During Noah's day, the Lord saw that the evil had gone too far. God didn't want anyone to perish, but he cannot let sin flourish in the earth. *"And the LORD said, My spirit shall not always strive with man . . . And GOD saw that the wickedness of man was great in the earth, and that every imagination of the thoughts of his heart was only evil continually. And it repented the LORD that he had made man on the earth, and it grieved him at his heart. And the LORD said, I will destroy man whom I have created from the face of the earth; both man, and beast, and the creeping thing, and the fowls of the air; for it repenteth me that I have made them. But Noah found grace in the eyes of the LORD* (Genesis 6:3, 5-8)." God told Noah that he was going to destroy man because of his violence. He commanded Noah to build an ark for his family and two of every animal of the earth, and God would make his covenant with them. Noah did as the Lord commanded. It rained forty days and forty nights. The waters prevailed for one hundred fifty days (Genesis 7:12, 24), destroying every living creature except for Noah and those who were in the ark with him.

After flood, God blessed Noah and his sons saying, *"Be fruitful, and multiply, and replenish the earth . . . behold, I establish my covenant with you, and with your seed after you; And with every living creature that is with you, of the fowl, of the cattle, and of every beast of the earth with you; from all that go out of the ark, to every beast of the earth. And I will establish my covenant with you; neither shall all flesh be cut off any more by the waters of a flood; neither shall there any more be a flood to destroy the earth* (Genesis 9:1-11)." The sons of Noah were, Shem, Ham and Japheth. All human beings of the earth were descendants of Noah's sons who became fruitful and multiplied across the face of the earth (Genesis 9:19), but before that happened, there was yet another rebellion.

Sometime after the flood, Noah grew a vineyard. One day Noah got drunk on wine, and fell down naked. Instead of covering up his father's nakedness, Ham made fodder and told his brothers. Shem and Japheth honored their father by walking backwards towards Noah and covering him with a garment. They did not see their father's nakedness. When Noah sobered from the wine and found out what Ham did, he cursed Ham's son Canaan. At first glance, this seems unfair, but it was the mercy of God that Noah did not curse Ham for what he did. If Ham had been cursed, then all of his sons, Egypt, Put, Cush and Canaan would have also been cursed. Noah blessed Shem. Japheth was to dwell with Shem. Canaan was to be the servant of them all. (Genesis 9:24-27). It was from Canaan's curse that the seeds of rebellion against God were sown.

Now, before I get deeper into this discussion about the Babylonian rebellion, I want to speak to a doctrine that is preached in some churches concerning Noah's curse of Canaan. Noah's sons represent every nation of people of this earth. There are some preachers who say that all Black people are cursed because Cush that was cursed. That is not so. It was

Canaan who was cursed. Canaan's descendants were all the "ites" during Moses' day when the Children of Israel (Shem's descendants) went to possess the Promised Land. *"And Canaan begat Sidon his firstborn, and Heth, And the Jebusite, and the Amorite, and the Girgasite, And the Hivite, and the Arkite, and the Sinite, And the Arvadite, and the Zemarite, and the Hamathite: and afterward were the families of the Canaanites spread abroad. And the border of the Canaanites was from Sidon, as thou comest to Gerar, unto Gaza; as thou goest, unto Sodom, and Gomorrah, and Admah, and Zeboim, even unto Lasha* (Genesis 10:15-19)." Biblical genealogies are very important. You will find that those whom were cursed by their father, will show up as the adversaries of those who were blessed. In the case of Noah's son. The Canaanites became the adversaries, by reason of Ham's son Canaan being cursed by Noah. In fact, Canaan's son Heth is ancestor to the Hittites. In the Hebrew, Heth means *terror*. There are numerous mention of the sons of Heth, "sons of terror." Later in this book I will talk about the significant role that terrorism plays in these last days. For now, let us return to Ham's son Cush. He was not cursed. Neither were any of the African nations he begat. Cush begat Nimrod (the great-grand son of Noah) who is the person of interest in the Babylonian rebellion. *"And Cush begat Nimrod: he began to be a mighty one in the earth. He was a mighty hunter before the LORD: wherefore it is said, Even as Nimrod the mighty hunter before the LORD. And the beginning of his kingdom was Babel, and Erech, and Accad, and Calneh, in the land of Shinar. Out of that land went forth Asshur, and builded Nineveh, and the city of Rehoboth and Calah, and Resen between Nineveh and Calah: the same is a great city* (Genesis 10:8-12)." Nimrod was a builder of great cities. He was known as a mighty hunter who hunted both man and beast. He led the Babylonian rebellion against God.

Let's consider the possible motivations for his rebellion, for therein we will learn much about why man rebel against God today. The Blessing Noah spoke over his sons still affect the nations of our world. Canaan may have been cursed, but Noah said nothing about Ham, his father. It was as though Ham did not exist and neither did his other sons Cush, Egypt and Put. These are the sons that would arise in rebellion. They knew that God blessed all the sons, and would not rest without establishing their right to their inheritance. If they could not get it God's way, they were determined to get it any way they could. This is the essence of the Babylonian spirit.

Here is the story of the Tower of Babel as told by the Bible. *"And the whole earth was of one language, and of one speech. And it came to pass, as they journeyed from the east, that they found a plain in the land of Shinar; and they dwelt there. And they said one to another, Go to, let us make brick, and burn them throughly. And they had brick for stone, and slime had they for morter. And they said, Go to, let us build us a city and a tower, whose top [may reach] unto heaven; and let us make us a name, lest we be scattered abroad upon the face of the whole earth. And the LORD came down to see the city and the tower, which the children of men builded. And the LORD said, Behold, the people [is] one, and they have all one language; and this they begin to do: and now nothing will be restrained from them, which they have imagined to do. Go to, let us go down, and there confound their language, that they may not understand one another's speech. So the LORD scattered them abroad from thence upon the face of all the earth: and they left off to build the city. Therefore is the name of it called Babel; because the LORD did there confound the language of all the earth: and from thence did the LORD scatter them abroad upon the face of all the earth* (Genesis 11:1-9).*"*

This is a short story that has left a powerful imprint on the human soul. The church focuses on Adam's sin, and rightfully so. It is what the Apostle Paul focused on when preaching to the Gentile churches. When the Lord began unfolding this message for today's church, he took me past Adam to the rebellion in heaven. Although Adam's sin was willful, he had no clue that his actions would curse the entire human race. Nimrod, on the hand, knew exactly what he was doing. He was indeed a mighty warrior before God. He was also an insurrectionist. Like Satan, Nimrod wanted to build his own kingdom. He obviously possessed the same powers of persuasion because Nimrod convinced the others to follow his rebellion against God. He turned their hearts away from God to do their own thing. They didn't want to disperse throughout the world as God commanded. They wanted to demonstrate a show of force against God. Jewish historian Flavius Josephus, recorded how God commanded the people more than once to disperse throughout the world and they would not. Some had fear of being in the lower elevations because of the flood.[1] Eventually, they traveled from Mount Ararat (In Turkey, near Iran) where the ark had landed and traveled west to the plains of Shinar (possibly near present day Bagdad). Josephus also wrote about how

---

1   Josephus, Flavius. "The Antiquities Of The Jews, Book I. Chapter 4. Concerning The Tower Of Babylon, And The Confusion Of Tongues."*The Complete Works Of Favius Josephus*.NA.

the generations were increasing and they flourished with young. This should have been confirmation that it was time to disperse, but they did not.² Not even calamities brought on by their disobedience dissuaded them. One would suppose that this was a close knit family that loved one another, after all they had no one else. They probably felt that there was safety in numbers, but they also knew they would incur the wrath of God.

Under the leadership of Nimrod, the people built a city and a tower as a defense against God. Here is a quote from Josephus: *"Now it was Nimrod who excited them to such an affront and contempt of God . . . He persuaded them not to ascribe it to God, as if it was through his means they were happy, but to believe that it was their own courage which procured that happiness. He also gradually changed the government into tyranny, seeing no other way of turning men from the fear of God, but to bring them into a constant dependence on his power. He also said he would be revenged on God, if he should have a mind to drown the world again; for that he would build a tower too high for the waters to be able to reach! And that he would avenge himself on God for destroying their forefathers!"³* This was a rather bold rebellion against God. The people actually believed that they could carry out such actions. What was it that made them think they had the power to withstand God? What had they seen and understood that made them so bold? These were men who knew that God gave them dominion over the earth. Did they actually think they could subdue their Creator as if he were just another creature like them? They witnessed God's power during the flood, and yet they were hardened against him. How does one take revenge on God without destroying himself? In any case, the tower was the plan they would have executed if God had not intervened. They had the power of agreement and thought they had power to overthrow Go. *"And I will give unto thee the keys of the kingdom of heaven: and whatsoever thou shalt bind on earth shall be bound in heaven: and whatsoever thou shalt loose on earth shall be loosed in heaven* (Matthew 16:19)." There was one minor problem. They tried to bind up God's plan for mankind, and that was not going to happen. So, God confused their language and scattered them over the face of the earth as he originally planned.

2	Josephus, Flavius. "The Antiquities Of The Jews, Book I. Chapter 4. Concerning The Tower Of Babylon, And The Confusion Of Tongues."*The Complete Works Of Favius Josephus*.NA.
3	Josephus, Flavius. "The Antiquities Of The Jews, Book I. Chapter 4. Concerning The Tower Of Babylon, And The Confusion Of Tongues."*The Complete Works Of Favius Josephus*.NA.

Let me share with you how the Lord specifically compares the Tower of Babel to the Christian Church in America. First of all, just like the people of Babel, the church has refused to go into all the world with the Gospel of the Kingdom. Remember that we learned that the Blessing and the message of the gospel are one in the same. It is just being told from two different perspectives, but the message is the same. We also talked about God's original plan to give an inheritance to his family. If was first given to Adam, but he lost it through sin. Then the Lord gave the inheritance to Noah and his sons after the flood. God Blessed them and told them to propagate the Blessing around the world. Shem obeyed, but Ham and Japheth refused because they were determined to fortify their position by building the Tower of Babel. So, God still could not get the message around the entire world because his people had another agenda. According to the Lord, they wanted to keep the message all to themselves. It was never about them, it was about God's original plan to reach the entire world.

Later in history, the descendants of Shem (the Jews) would do the same. The Jews during Jesus' day did not want to take the message of the Kingdom to the Gentiles. The prophets spoke about God's people being a light to the Gentiles (Isaiah 49:6-7). God wanted to Bless the world, the Jews hid that message. The Psalmist captured the benefits of the Blessing, *"Bless the LORD, O my soul: and all that is within me, [bless] his holy name. Bless the LORD, O my soul, and forget not all his benefits: Who forgiveth all thine iniquities; who healeth all thy diseases; Who redeemeth thy life from destruction; who crowneth thee with lovingkindness and tender mercies; Who satisfieth thy mouth with good [things; so that] thy youth is renewed like the eagle's. The LORD executeth righteousness and judgment for all that are oppressed. He made known his ways unto Moses, his acts unto the children of Israel. The LORD [is] merciful and gracious, slow to anger, and plenteous in mercy* (Psalm 103:1-8).*"* These benefits were not just for the Jews, God executes righteousness and justice **for all** who are oppressed in the earth. This is the light the Gentiles needed to see. The Jews knew about the Blessing, but they were distracted by their own desire for a Messiah.

God promised through the prophets, to raise up an earthly King of the Jews (Isaiah 9:6). They wanted their own king and their own kingdom. Their religious traditions became a pseudo kingdom in which they could separate themselves from the Gentiles. Now, when Jesus came preaching *"The Kingdom of God is within you* (Luke 17:21),*"* the Jews rejected the notion that he could be their Messiah. They expected to see a kingdom that would overtake Rome in their day. Even after his resurrection, Jesus appeared to the apostles and they still did understand. *"When they therefore were come together, they asked of him, saying, Lord, wilt thou at this time restore again the kingdom to Israel* (Acts 1:6)*?"* Jesus responded, *"It is not for you to know the times or the seasons, which the Father hath put in his own power. But ye shall receive power, after that the Holy Ghost is come upon you: and ye shall be witnesses unto me both in Jerusalem, and in all Judaea, and in Samaria, and unto the uttermost part of the earth* (Acts 1:7-8).*"* In other words, Jesus told them not to be concern about when the Kingdom would be restored. Instead they were to witness to the Jews and to the entire world about the resurrection. The power of the resurrection was the message they were to deliver to the world; a power available to all who would believe. Did the apostles go? No, not immediately. It wasn't until the stoning of Stephan that they would obey Jesus' command to leave Jerusalem (Acts 8:1). God allowed persecution to come upon the apostles. This is what forced them to obey Jesus' command to take the message to the world. Eventually, they all left Jerusalem, but only under threat of severe persecution.

They all left, but it was with much controversy amongst the Jews. They had forgotten the words of the prophets. *"And he said, It is a light thing that thou shouldest be my servant to raise up the tribes of Jacob, and to restore the preserved of Israel: I will also give thee for a light to the Gentiles, that thou mayest be my salvation unto the end of the earth* (Isaiah 49:6).*"* Salvation was to be sent to the world. It started with the Jews because of the Blessing that God promised Abraham. What was that Blessing? *"In blessing I will bless thee, and in multiplying I will multiply thy seed as the stars of the heaven, . . . And in thy seed shall all the nations of the earth be blessed; because thou hast obeyed my voice* (Genesis 22:17-18).*"* Abraham was told that in his seed, all the nations of the earth would be blessed. Here is the significance of this Blessing. We learned earlier that God Blessed Noah and his sons, Shem Japheth and Ham. Noah made the decision to pass the Blessing to Shem. That is how the Blessing came to Abraham. He was in the lineage of Shem. We can trace this same Blessing all the way back to Adam and his sons, Cain, Abel and Seth. We did not discuss the sons, but most people know that Cain killed his brother Abel (Genesis 4:8). If the Blessing had been in operation then, it would have gone to Adam's son Abel. After he was killed, it went to Seth. As his names indicates, he was the *substitute seed* to replace Abel. The Bible says that when Seth bore his son Enos, men began again to call upon the Lord again (Genesis 4:25-26). Noah was from the lineage of Enos. God returned the Blessing to Noah, but this was not because there were no good people before Noah. There were good men. The most notable was Enoch, the father of Methuselah and grandfather of Noah. Here is what the Bible says, *"And Enoch walked with God after he begat Methuselah three hundred years, and begat sons and daughters: And all the days of Enoch were three hundred sixty and five years: And Enoch walked with God: and he was not; for God took him (Genesis 5:21-24)."* Enoch was so pleasing to God, that God took him to heaven. Obviously Noah had a wonderful example to follow, but it was more than that. This was Noah's destiny. Lamech, the son of Methuselah had a son, *"And he called his name Noah, saying, This same shall comfort us concerning our work and toil of our hands, because of the ground which the LORD hath cursed (Genesis 5:29)."* The ground had been cursed since Adam's sin. The sons of Seth saw Noah's birth as a sign that God would once again comfort his people. Indeed they were correct, but that comfort would only come after God brought great pain and suffering upon the earth, when he sent the flood waters.

Here is the thing to note. Israel is *Semitic*; meaning from the lineage of Noah's son Shem. God used the Jews, but the message of the gospel (the Blessing) was always meant for the whole world. It was never God's plan to isolate one race or nation in favor of another. God needed a family to begin with. He choose Noah and Abraham, just like he chose Adam, but God made it clear that he would use their families to reach the world. He did the same in choosing Abraham. God made their families a sign to the world. The Blessing they walked in, God would make available to all who would obey. No matter whom he uses, we must not forget that God is just using us. His plan is bigger than any one nation or people. Here is God's ultimate plan for all men. *"And they sung a new song, saying, Thou art worthy to take the book, and to open the seals thereof: for thou wast slain, and hast redeemed us to God by thy blood <u>out of every kindred, and tongue, and people, and nation</u>; And hast made us unto our God kings and priests: and we shall reign on the earth (Revelation 5:9-10)."* Here is yet another witness of God's plan for all men, *"After this I beheld, and, lo, a great multitude, which no man could number, <u>of all nations, and kindreds, and people, and tongues, stood before the throne, and before the Lamb</u>, clothed with* *white robes, and palms in their hands; And cried with a loud voice, saying, Salvation to our God which sitteth upon the throne, and unto the Lamb* (Revelation 7:9-10)." How about one more witness to God's plan? *"And I saw another angel fly in the midst of heaven, having the everlasting gospel <u>to preach unto them that dwell on the earth, and to every nation, and kindred, and tongue, and people</u>, Saying with a loud voice, Fear God, and give glory to him; for the hour of his judgment is come: and worship him that made heaven, and earth, and the sea, and the fountains of waters* (Revelation 14:6-7)."

In this last passage, God has an angel preaching the gospel to every nation, kindred, tongue and people. The gospel was not just for the Jew. It is not just for the church. God's original plan was for the Blessing to go to all the people of the world. The apostles were told to preach the gospel to the Gentile nations of the world. Who were these people? Those of the lineage of Japheth and Ham, all of the Gentile nations of the world came from these two sons of Noah. This is why as believers, we cannot afford to make enemies of any nation of the earth. You cannot reach a people group that you consider evil or unclean. Let's recall what happened to Peter when God sent him to a Gentile home. Cornelius was a Gentile who was faithful in prayer and giving to the work of the Lord. The angel appeared to him telling him to send men to find Peter. Then, the Lord also appeared to Peter in a vision., *"Heaven opened, and a certain vessel descending unto him, as it had been a great sheet knit at the four corners, and let down to the earth: Wherein were all manner of fourfooted beasts of the earth, and wild beasts, and creeping things, and fowls of the air. And there came a voice to him, Rise, Peter; kill, and eat. But Peter said, Not so, Lord; for I have never eaten any thing that is common or unclean. And the voice [spake] unto him again the second time, What God hath cleansed, [that] call not thou common. This was done thrice: and the vessel was received up again into heaven* (Acts 10:1-48)." While Peter was trying to figure out what all of this meant, the men Cornelius sent arrived at the house looking for him. Peter went to their home and shared the gospel. The Holy Ghost fell upon them all and they got saved, baptized and filled with the spirit. God was confirming that the Blessing was also for the Gentiles, but the Jews were not pleased when they heard what Peter had done. The Gentiles were considered unclean to the Jews. Not only did Peter go to a Gentile home, but stayed there a few days and ate with them. This was not allowed under Jewish law. We see the same attitudes in the church today. They refuse to go to certain people groups because of prejudiced attitudes. God still has a message to deliver to the entire world. Oftentimes, he has to take the message and give it to someone more faithful to carry out kingdom instructions. We saw this with the ancient Jews. When they did not take the message to the Gentiles, Jesus raised up the Church to take it to the world. Not the modern Church refuses to take the message to all the sectors of the world. They simply refuse to go to some places.

Why won't the church work the ministry of Jesus Christ the way He commanded? The Lord says that **the church is operating in fear of the world**. That is why they refused to go into the world and preach the gospel. There is a spirit of isolation, or better yet a *spirit of division* that is causing them to view the world as "those people." Consequently, Christian parents refuse to send their children to public schools or colleges fearing that they would be brainwashed against their faith. This fear stems from a basic lack of knowledge of who they are In Christ. Is Christ so weak that we have to fear mixing with people unlike us? This is wrong! God's people are being destroyed for the lack of this knowledge (Hosea 4:6). It's not like they don't know what the Bible says, they just have another mind that replaces the mind of Christ. Instead of moving out into the world like a mighty army, the American Church acts like it is afraid of contamination from the world. It's as if they do not believe the word of God that says, *"Ye are of God, little children, and have overcome them: because greater is he that is in you, than he that is in the world* (I John 4:4)."

While Jesus is saying, *"Go Ye,"* the church is not responding as they should. Sure, there are some who are obeying the call, but they are far and in between. Rather than standing up to the world in dominion, the church is retreating from its duty to save the world. Many of the church sees the world as the greater influence in our nation; a giant too powerful to conquer on its own. This grasshopper mentality has destroyed the power of the church. Jesus didn't tell the church to go alone. All they have to do is obey the command to go, and the Lord promises to back up what they do with signs following (Mark 16:20). Disobedience and unbelief is naturally accepted in the church. The American Church is refusing to go to the Gentiles, and for similar reasons as the Jews. Who are we to call someone else unclean or unworthy of God's Blessing? It is the Grace of God that has to be made available for all men. Remember that it was (and still is) God's desire to have one family; one people being one in heart and speaking the same thing, but not just speaking what they want to speak. God wanted them to speak His words in the earth. We got a glimpse of such a family in the upper room when the Holy Ghost came and the one hundred twenty began speaking in tongues. They were in agreement with each other, **and** in agreement with God. They were one with God. *"And when the day of Pentecost was fully come, they were all with one accord in one place. And suddenly there came a sound from heaven as of a rushing mighty wind, and it filled all the house where they were sitting. And there appeared unto them cloven tongues like as of fire, and it sat upon each of them. And they were all filled with the Holy Ghost, and began to speak with other tongues, as the Spirit gave them utterance* (Acts 2:1-4)." They were all speaking the words of God in unknown tongues. In fact, speaking in tongues is one of the best ways to converse with God. Since you don't know what you are saying, you have no opportunity to argue with God. On the other hand, the Holy Spirit speaks those things that we cannot speak in our understanding. He will only speak the will of God for our lives. *"Likewise the Spirit also helpeth our infirmities: for we know not what we should pray for as we ought: but the Spirit itself maketh intercession for us with groanings which cannot be uttered. And he that searcheth the hearts knoweth what [is] the mind of the Spirit, because he maketh intercession for the saints according to [the will of] God* (Romans 8:26-27)." Jesus wanted us to be one, as he and the Father were one (John 17:20-22). It's that oneness with God that is the answer to the prayer Jesus prayed to the Father.

We mentioned how the American Church is one with all its members against the plan of God, but the Lord revealed another pattern of rebellious behavior that goes back to Noah and his sons. The Lord said that men tend to treat God as if he were just a man like themselves. *"God is not a man, that he should lie; neither the son of man, that he should repent: hath he said, and shall he not do it? Or hath he spoken, and shall he not make it good* (Numbers 23:19)?" They don't seem to understand that God could never be like us. He does not have the sin nature in him. We were originally created in the image and likeness of God, but Adam sinned causing all men to be born under a curse. God is perfect. There is no iniquity in him. God is pure and holy. Years ago, the Lord explained to me that there was only one thing he **could not** do. He said, **"I cannot violate my word."** Whatever God speaks, has to come to pass, and no one can stop it. The Isaiah wrote beautiful words that describes how

God's word must come to pass. *"For as the rain cometh down, and the snow from heaven, and returneth not thither, but watereth the earth, and maketh it bring forth and bud, that it may give seed to the sower, and bread to the eater: So shall my word be that goeth forth out of my mouth: it shall not return unto me void, but it shall accomplish that which I please, and it shall prosper in the thing whereto I sent it* (Isaiah 55:10-11).*"* God speaks things into the earth that he wants to come to pass. If he didn't want it, God would have never spoken it. Now, let us once again consider how God Blessed Noah and his sons (Genesis 9:1). In the eyes of God, the Blessing was great enough for not only Noah's sons, but for every son that would be born in the generations to come. Noah took it upon himself to pass the Blessing only to Shem (Genesis 9:26). Noah determined that only one son was eligible for **that** which God gave to them all. Noah chose to favor one son over the others. This same pattern can be seen throughout the Bible, as the fathers determine who gets the Blessing. ***Earthly fathers choose favorites, God does not.*** He sees us all as his firstborn sons. That is why we are joint heirs with Jesus (Romans 8:16-17) and not second, third or fourth in line for the inheritance. With God, there is no difference between his sons.

One of the reasons that terrorism will increase in the last days is because the Sons of God will be coming forth in the earth. As they step into their inheritance, it will cause others to be jealous. They will be tempted to steal, even kill to take from those whom God has Blessed. Again, it is because men are told that God has made a difference between his sons. Well, he has, but not in the way men think. God gave one requirement for the Blessing: obedience. Obedience is all that is required, but evil men refuse to obey and yet they want the Blessing of God. That will not happen. It is not God who is making a difference between his sons. It is that one son is cooperate with God for the Blessing and the other son will not. God cannot violate his word and the evil son will not obey. They will be at an impasse until the rebellious son determines to obey. God will not be moved. Now, the evil son can choose to do what Cain did and kill his brother, but that will only bring the curse and death upon his own life. Either way, God's will cannot be circumvented.

Now, there is also the Babylonian opinion that because we are human beings, we are all entitled to God's Blessing. If sin and death had not entered into the earth, every human would have been born into the family of God and entitled to this inheritance. That was not what happened.

Adam's sin cut us off from the Blessing and caused every human to be born into the curse and death. God never wanted man to be cursed or to die. So, what would he have done if man had never sinned and death had never entered into the world? What would God have done if the earth had been fully populated with his heirs? I believe that he would have started populating the other planets and galaxies with his heirs. God is ever increasing. He does not plan for lack or decline. He and everything he creates keeps expanding (multiplying and replenishing). This is an ordinary effect of the Blessing. If God had so many heirs, that they filled up every planet and galaxy, I believe that he would simply create more planets and galaxies, just for the pleasure of Blessing his sons and daughters. There is no limit to God's resources or his love for his creation. This is the nature of God.

There is no lack in God, or in his plan for mankind. If there is no lack or limitation in God, where did lack come from? Lack is a perception that humans have created in this world. It is a perception that is based in fear. In fact, the entire world operates in fear. Remember Nimrod using the people's fear of another flood as a reason to build the tower? He used fear to gather the people under one cohesive plan to get revenge on God. Isn't this the same strategy that the serpent used on Eve? He tried to plant the seeds of fear in her mind; that God could not be trusted; that he was with holding something good from them. This was a lie. She nor Adam lacked nothing. They had an infinite source of good everything in garden. People have a limited understanding of how God designed this world. This limitation causes them to fear, unnecessarily. God has all the answers. Whatever we need to know, all we need to do is ask him (James 1:5). God's wisdom is infinite. Has any human created the heavens and ruled the earth? Did we create the law of gravity? Did we cause seedtime and harvest to enter the earth? Did we create the sun, the moon or the stars? We didn't create any of these things, God did. He made these things for our benefit. God is good father. Children who know and love their fathers, don't rebel against them. They try their best to please their fathers in every way. Obedience is the key indicator that someone belongs to God. If we love him, then we obey him (John 14:23). Until you receive Jesus Christ, you are not capable of loving or obeying God. You must be born again. The sin nature has to be dealt with. Man cannot do it alone. We are not even inclined to deal with sin because it seems so natural to us. It is natural in a cursed world, but it's not of God.

The heavenly Father loved us so much that he sent Jesus to take care of the sin issue for us. It's really a fool proof plan that leads us back to the Blessing. We need only accept Jesus and let the Holy Spirit lead us to God's divine plan for their lives. Everyone who comes to Christ has the power to become sons of God (John 1:12), but only those who are led by the Holy Spirit will actually manifest the inheritance as sons. As they follow the Lord, they will learn to walk just like Adam did before the fall, and just like Jesus walked in this earth.

Obedient sons imitate their fathers (Ephesians 5:1). God requires that we walk in love, just as Jesus loved us and gave his life for us. Being a member of a church does not automatically qualify you as a son of God. You must be born again into God's family. You must have received Jesus and made God your father. This has to be done by faith. Everything in God's kingdom is obtained by faith alone. The Apostle Paul spoke about a similar issue as concerning the Jews of his day. He said that not all of Israel is the rightful seed. According to Paul, only those who walked in the faith like Abraham would qualified as heir (Romans 4:16). How did Abraham walk? Abraham walked by faith, the same way that Jesus walked. He heard the voice of God and did whatever God said do. Again, God wants a family that is operating with one heart, speaking His words and doing His works in the earth. Doing the religious thing disqualifies you. Doing **your own** thing automatically disqualifies you. You must be connected by God's spirit and be walking by faith. For example, King Solomon didn't get a free ride because he was David's son. *"He shall build an house for my name, and I will establish the throne of his kingdom for ever. I will be his father, and he shall be my son. If he commit iniquity, I will chasten him with the rod of men, and with the stripes of the children of men: But my mercy shall not depart away from him, as I took it from Saul, whom I put away before thee. And thine house and thy kingdom shall be established for ever before thee: thy throne shall be established for ever* (II Samuel 7:13-16).*"*

David charged Solomon to build the house of the Lord, and he gave his son powerful advice for keeping his inheritance in God. *"Now, my son, the LORD be with thee; and prosper thou, and build the house of the LORD thy God, as he hath said of thee. Only the LORD give thee wisdom and understanding, and give thee charge concerning Israel, that thou mayest keep the law of the LORD thy God. Then shalt thou prosper, if thou takest heed to fulfil the statutes and judgments which the LORD charged Moses with concerning Israel: be strong, and of good courage; dread not, nor be dismayed* (I Chronicles 22:11-13)." Notice anything familiar about those last few words David spoke to his son? They sound like the same words God spoke to Joshua when he was about to take charge after Moses' death (Joshua 1:7). He was about to lead the people to possess the land on the other side of Jordan. I'm hearing something else in the spirit. **Just because we know what God promises, does not mean we know how he will bring it to pass.** If his promise is to the Jews, that means all Jews are eligible, but only the obedient ones will obtain it. I know this sounds repetitive, but the Lord is putting it in my spirit to express once again, but in another way. I recall a statement John the Baptist spoke to the Jewish leaders who refused to repent. They claimed that because they were the seed of Abraham, they had no need to repent. John spoke these profound words, *"Bring forth therefore fruits worthy of repentance, and begin not to say within yourselves, We have Abraham to our father: for I say unto you, That God is able of these stones to raise up children unto Abraham* (Luke 3:8)." I also recall the time when Jesus rode into town on the colt and the people were shouting, *"Saying, Blessed be the King that cometh in the name of the Lord: peace in heaven, and glory in the highest."* The Pharisees told Jesus to rebuke his disciples for hailing him as King. Jesus cleverly replied, *"I tell you that, if these should hold their peace, the stones would immediately cry out* (Luke 19:37-40)."

Too often God's people get full of themselves, thinking that God cannot do without them. That is far from the truth. God graces us with the opportunity to be his heirs. If he can command stones to take our place, then God clearly does not need us, but he **does** desire that we come freely in faith and obedience. He uses us, but it is not about us. Let us see how this was demonstrated in the life of Solomon. God made Solomon the greatest king in wisdom and in riches, but he still violated one the most important laws Moses gave the people concerning marriage. They were not allow to marry those who worshipped strange gods (Deuteronomy 7:3,4). *"But king Solomon loved many strange women, together with the daughter of Pharaoh, women of the Moabites, Ammonites, Edomites, Zidonians, and Hittites; Of the nations concerning which the LORD said unto the children of Israel, Ye shall not go in to them, neither shall they come in unto you: for surely they will turn away your heart after their gods: Solomon clave unto these in love. And he had seven hundred wives, princesses, and three hundred concubines:*

and his wives turned away his heart. For it came to pass, when Solomon was old, that his wives turned away his heart after other gods: and his heart was not perfect with the LORD his God, as was the heart of David his father (I Kings 11:1-4)." God was angry with Solomon and tried to reason with him twice, but he would not heed the word of the Lord. *"Wherefore the LORD said unto Solomon, Forasmuch as this is done of thee, and thou hast not kept my covenant and my statutes, which I have commanded thee, I will surely rend the kingdom from thee, and will give it to thy servant. Notwithstanding in thy days I will not do it for David thy father's sake: but I will rend it out of the hand of thy son. Howbeit I will not rend away all the kingdom; but will give one tribe to thy son for David my servant's sake, and for Jerusalem's sake which I have chosen* (I Kings 11:9-13)." So what did God do? He stirred up enemies against Solomon. God also chose one of the king's servants Jeroboam, and made him king over ten tribes and left one tribe for Solomon's son Rehoboam. For the first time, Israel was divided into nations. Jeroboam was King of Israel and Rehoboam was King of Judah. These kings warred against each other all the days of their reign. Both kings departed from the ways of King David and did much evil in the sight of God, causing the people to also sin against God (I Kings 11; 12; 13).

This battle over the throne is just an extension of the battle over the inheritance. Again, the blood line inheritance was for the heirs of David, but Solomon's rebellion cut off his heirs from receiving their full inheritance. It was given to another. God cannot reward sin, even if by blood the person is entitled. In fact, God said, *"The soul that sinneth, it shall die* (Ezekiel 18:20)." That is what God told Adam. Death may not be immediate. It can be long and agonizing, causing men to suffer greatly. It gives God no pleasure that his creation suffers, but he gave us the choice. *"I call heaven and earth to record this day against you, that I have set before you life and death, blessing and cursing: therefore choose life, that both thou and thy seed may live: That thou mayest love the LORD thy God, and that thou mayest obey his voice, and that thou mayest cleave unto him: for he is thy life, and the length of thy days: that thou mayest dwell in the land which the LORD sware unto thy fathers, to Abraham, to Isaac, and to Jacob, to give them* (Deuteronomy 30:19-20)." God gave us a choice that included enjoying the Blessing and possessing the land he promised. He only required that we love and obey him. That is **the only** requirement for obtaining God's inheritance, yet it is the very thing men fight against. We want the Blessing, but we don't want to obey the One who made us his heir. Men won't obey God, but they will fight their brothers to the death, in an attempt to keep them from receiving their inheritance. Again, earthly men are limited in their understanding. They think the inheritance is about a person, or about a position. When God has generations on his mind. God is looking at posterity. ***Many people and generations are connected to a single act of obedience.*** When we obey God, it changes the spiritual atmosphere from the curse to the Blessing, which causes a chain reaction of goodness and prosperity to fall upon the lives of those around us. The Blessing greatly enhances lives and changes how future generations will develop. Men are short-sighted. They only see themselves. It's not about us. Get over yourselves! It is about the mission and the message. God wants to reach the world, but men refuse to go. If you talk to the average preacher in America, they would say they are doing a terrific job for the kingdom. Babylonian churches are doing what they always do. They are doing their own thing, not even aware that there is a real game going on in the spirit; unaware that there is a great cloud of witnesses in the stands watching it all. They are waiting for the game to get going. So, we have to get rid of sin and anything that is hindering God's team from getting into position and winning this game (Hebrews 12:1-2). We cannot win looking at other people and what they are doing. We have to look to Jesus. He chose us for his team and expects us to stay in our position.

Will this rebellion ever end? Well, we know from prophecy that God's team wins. Who is remaining on the field when that trumpet sounds, is yet to be determined. The Babylonian system in America began with an organized rebellion against God, and it has become a way of life. Preachers will say that the Babylonian spirit is political, but God says ***it is a reflection of the spiritual rebellion of the American Church. It's a evil Christian harvest, a bad crop that must be destroyed if God's will is to be done.*** As with any harvest, if you want a different crop, you have to plant (sow) a different seed. That means rooting out, and pulling down, and destroying, and throwing down, rebuilding, and planting the desired seed (Jeremiah 1:10). Jesus said,*"Every plant, which my heavenly Father hath not planted, shall be rooted up* (Matthew 15:13)." The evil Christian harvest has to be uprooted. The evil trees and its fruit must be cut down and burned. *"Repent ye: for the kingdom of heaven is at hand . . . And now also the axe is laid unto the root of the trees: therefore every tree which bringeth not forth good fruit is hewn down,* *and cast into the fire* (Matthew 3:1, 10)." This is the message that John the Baptist preached right before Jesus came to begin his ministry. It is the same message God is speaking to his church today. Jesus is about to return, and we are not ready. The church is not ready. The nations are not ready because the church has not done what God commanded. The American Church has been too busy doing its own thing. We have to get back on track and get ready. There needs to be an uprooting of our own ideas. We need to cast down all imaginations and every high thought that exalts itself above that which God has commanded for his church. We need to bring every thought into the obedience of Christ (II Corinthians 10:5). We need to check our hearts and our motivations. Not every good idea is God ordained. God is very strategic. He typically goes against the grain. Popular opinions mean nothing to God. He does not take the obvious path to get something done. He directs us to the path that is most effective for the Kingdom. It's a narrow path. To get back on the path with God, we need the thoughts of God. We need to follow the ways of God. How do we do this? We need a revelation from heaven. First and foremost we need wisdom and revelation in the knowledge of Jesus Christ. We also need to have a revelation of God's calling for our lives. We need to have a revelation of the inheritance he has for us. We need to have a revelation of the greatness of his power that has been given to those of us who believe (Ephesians 1:17-19). This kind of revelation requires that we have an intimate relationship with our Lord. Jesus said, *"And this is life eternal, that they might know thee the only true God, and Jesus Christ, whom thou hast sent* (John 17:3)."

Most Christians think eternal life is something you get when you go to heaven. Not True. Eternal life is the intimate knowledge of the Father and the son. It is a relationship that results from spending time in the Bible and in prayer. It is when we allow the Holy Spirit to reveal heaven's secrets to our hearts. Then you will learn about God's great plan for your life. It is exceedingly abundantly more than you could ask or think, but you can only obtain it according to how much you allow the Holy Spirit to work in your life (Ephesians 3:20). The Holy Spirit really bothers some Christians. They love getting revelation, but listening and obeying the Holy Spirit is another thing. He may tell you so sow (give) something into someone's life. He may direct you to pickup and go to a new city; even to an environment that is not pleasing to you. Remember what Jesus did for us. He left the beauty and peace of Heaven to come to this dying world. Jesus got on a cross and died for sins he never committed, and you are complaining about what God wants you to do? Whether you choose to obey or not, someone else's life will be affected. There are people dying in poverty because someone **God called** would not go. The Blessing comes to replenish whatever is lacking in our human lives. God places those answers within the hearts of his people, to be executed in this earth. If we hear and don't obey, the cure is not found and the condition is not changed. There are missionaries in the field doing their best, but without being led by the Spirit of God, they will always fall short. God designed this world to function by his spirit. Even the world's secrets belong to God. He reveals those secrets only to his children (Deuteronomy 29:29). This is part of our inheritance. I asked the Lord once, why it was that poverty was not decreasing in the world. He told me that he had people in America who would not go and do what he commanded them to do in those nations. The Babylonian system would say that there is a shortage of money and resources. According to God, ***"There is no lack of resources, only a lack of obedient people who are willing to share their time and resources with others."***

The spirit of Babylon tells men that it is all about them; that they have to build something of note to make their names great. All God is asking is for his people to hear his voice and obey his spirit. He will give us notable things to do, and he will make our names great. If you want the Blessing of Abraham, you have to do what Abraham did. He heard the voice of God and obeyed. He left all that he knew and followed the Lord to an unknown land in search of his promise. We are blessed today because of his obedience. Now it is our time to be obedient and bless all the nations of the world.

"Now the Lord said unto Abram, Get thee out of thy country, and from thy kindred, and from thy father's house, unto a land that I will shew thee. And I will make of thee a great nation, and I will bless thee, and make thy name great; and thou shalt be a blessing: and I will bless them that bless thee, and I will curse them who curseth thee; and in thee shall all the families of the earth shall be blessed." Genesis 12:1-3

The Unholy Trinity: Religion, Tradition, Commandments of Men

Christians all over the world are waiting for that glorious day, when the Lord will descend from the heavens with a shout, with the voice of the archangel and the sound of the trumpet. It's is the glorious day when the dead in Christ shall arise first, and those of us who are alive shall be caught up together with them in the clouds. It will be the day when that which is corruptible becomes incorruptible; when mortality puts on immortality. In a twinkling of the eye we shall all be changed. We will meet the Lord in the air, and forever shall be with Him. The Apostle Paul exhorted us to comfort each other with these words (I Thessalonians 4:16-18; I Corinthians 15:51-53). This will be the rapture of the Lord's church. The day in which God will remove the church from the earth, before the final days of tribulation; when all hell breaks lose.

We who are in Christ, look forward to this day, but the Spirit of the Lord says that we are not ready for our Lord's return. Jesus is coming back for a *"Glorious Church, not having spot, or wrinkle, or any such thing; but that is should be holy and without blemish (Ephesians 5:27)."* In America, the church has not done what God called it to do. We have taken the resurrection power out of the gospel, and have chosen religion instead. The church has also disregarded the role of the prophet and the apostles who are the prophetic and administrative voices of the church. What we have done, is nothing short of treasonous. We have purported to follow Jesus Christ, and yet the American Church was established in willful rebellion against Him. Here is a quote from the Holy Spirit, *"Jesus said that his church would be built upon the foundation of the apostles and prophets. Because American churches have eliminated these two foundational offices, his church was never built in our nation. Hearing this bothered me greatly. God was saying that the church structure we built in America is not his; it is a bastard. It is illegitimate as far as God is concerned. This is why so many Christians in America are not receiving their inheritance. They are not entitled, but the good news is that they can become legitimate today. They must turn from religion and turn back to loving God and obeying him. Then there is the aspect of kingdom dominion. The church in America as we know it, is not adept to handle the evil that is coming upon the earth in these last days. They will not be able to overcome without resurrection power. Unfortunately, they don't believe in the supernatural power of the Holy Ghost. They don't believe God speaks to men today. They don't even believe that apostles and prophets exist."*[1] There has been a constant pattern of behavior in the church. If they did not understand something in the Bible, they simply threw it out and made up their own doctrine. Without the Holy Spirit's guidance, no man can understand the Kingdom. The church at large does not believe in the Holy Spirit. Some are fearful of even talking about supernatural things, and yet it is the supernatural power of the Holy Spirit that was essential to everything Jesus and the apostles did. Jesus gave us power (Luke 10:19), yet church leaders never understood this Therefore they teach the Bible as a historical gospel that has little or no relevance in our day. This is preposterous! God's divine power has given us all things (all solutions and answers) that pertain to life and godliness (II Peter 1:3). The church has to understand this. People around us are suffering, but the church does not seem to notice. I pray that God opens their eyes (II Kings 6:17) to see that every solution we need is in the realm of the spirit. Without the anointing of the Holy Ghost, we cannot get those vital answers we need.

Look at Jesus. He was a man anointed with the Holy Ghost and power (Acts 10:38). Jesus went about doing good and healing all who were oppressed by the devil. He came to set them free; not in words only, but also in deed. Jesus fed the multitudes. He helped boost the fishing business, and he paid taxes supernaturally. He didn't send his followers to the federal government, Jesus gave them to eat. This was proof of the gospel. Where modern men could not produce the same results, they made up reasons why God does not do that thing any more. God never changed. Jesus Christ is the same, yesterday, today and forever (Hebrews 13:8). Modern men simply refuse to accept that supernatural things are real, **more real** than everything we see around us. It is common to hear leaders of the church say, "God does not do that any more." "Tongues don't exist any more." "The Holy Spirit and spiritual gifts are faded away." This is what religion does. It takes the truth of God and denies the power of its operation (II Timothy 3:5). Christianity's success is in one's faith that what God says is true. It's a faith that believes what Jesus did was real, and if he said we would do greater works, then so be it. With religion, people choose rituals such as prayer and fasting, communion and foot washing services and turned them into acts of piety.

---

[1]   Matthews, Paula. "The Call To Apostleship (Restoring God's Kingdom Dynasty)". *Jesus Gave Us Power Over Death*. Shaker Heights: Spirit & Life Publications[SM], 2014. 96. Print.

Few people even remember why Jesus did such things. They pray and fast with no results because they do so to satisfy their own desires and not to please God. I've known ministers who bragged about fasting for forty days like Jesus did. They bragged about their making it without food for forty days, yet they saw no spiritual results. Fasting was established by God, to afflict the human soul for the sake of loosening the bonds of wickedness, undoing heavy burdens and letting the oppressed go free. It was a fast to make one less focused on himself, and more focused on taking care of the needy and drawing near to those of his own family (Isaiah 58:6-7). Religion reduces the powerful ordinances of God down to weak hypocritical symbols. Because of the hypocritical nature of these rituals, it leads entire congregations to believe that God has no power, nor is he relevant in our day, when quite the opposite is true. When church leaders could not replicate the results of Jesus' ministry, they utilized rituals to make themselves feel holy. They also devised their own theories as to why God does not do the supernatural any more.

Let's take a look at prayer. Most people in the church pray, but they don't expect God to answer. So why do they do it? Because it is expected that good Christians should pray. I grew up in a Baptist church that believed in praying for the sick, but they did not believe God would heal. Instead they prayed and said, "If it is God's will, you will be healed." This bothered me as a child because why waste God's time with empty words if you do not expect him to answer? Then there was the manner in which they prayed. They didn't go boldly to the throne in their time of need (Hebrews 4:14-16). They had this sing-song manner praying that had nothing to do with the word or Jesus' power to heal. There was lots of drama, but no power. It was as if they were begging and crying and pleading with God to come down from heaven. They never even acknowledged the power of the Holy Spirit which was given to all believers. They just moaned and cried and screamed, hoping that if it was God's will, he would heal them.

I had a similar experience with some Catholic friends of mine. They were having an emergency prayer service and asked me to sit in and help them pray. I agreed, and to my surprise the nuns led prayer much like people in my Baptist church did. There was lots of emotion and everyone was crying out the name of Jesus and asking for his help. They needed him to give them an answer for a very specific problem. After about five minutes of prayer, I heard the Holy Spirit give the answer.

This was an encouraging prophetic word for this congregation. Since I didn't know how they would respond to a prophetic word, I asked the Lord if I should speak. He said no. When I asked why, he said because they did not expect a verbal answer from heaven. He said they would not receive the message because it was too supernatural for their understanding. Well, I sat through the prayer meeting, and stopped praying after the Lord gave the answer. It would have been hypocritical of me to keep praying to Jesus, and asking him the same thing over and over again, when the Holy Spirit had already given the answer. I have many loving Catholic friends who are into the ritual of rosary beads and their prayer book. They would prefer to say the appropriate number of *Hail Mary*'s rather to hear from God directly. Now, I did have one business associate who invited me to her Korean Charismatic Catholic service. It was heavenly. The service was performed in the Korean language, but I didn't care because the Holy Ghost was moving and love was in the air. It was a powerful service. The only odd thing for me was that the large cathedral was packed, and almost everyone was Korean and very short in stature. Of course, I stood out in the crowd, but no one seemed to notice because the glory cloud was heavy all around us. It indeed was a heavenly experience.

Religion uses ritual behavior, and creates a false sense of holiness and piety, but tradition is quite another thing. Tradition occurs when men decided to throw out God's commandment to do what they always been done in the past. I grew up in the Baptist Church. When it came to raising money, instead of sowing seed and reaping a financial harvest as the Bible prescribes, we had bake sales, fish and spaghetti dinners and car washes. We weren't taught Matthew 6:33, so no one knew to seek first the kingdom. Although these types of fund raisers were popular with all the local Baptist churches, but no one ever made any real money. Then there was the special event offerings when the deacons put a table at the front of the sanctuary and everyone walks by and places their offering on the table. The offerings were generally so small, that the deacons could count the money as people passed the table. They would announce how much they collected, and usually asked who was able to round it up to a larger figure. It was never very much money and quite embarrassing when this was to be the "love offering" for the guest speaker. Years later, I would be introduced to a similar tradition in the Pentecostal churches. So many of those so called *revivals*, where they bring in big named preachers for weekend or week long meeting, were not revivals at all. They were simply fund raising events. Now, remember we are talking about the Babylonian spirit in the church. This the spirit that rebels against God's command and it wants to do its own thing. Jesus said that men have made the word of God of no effect because of their traditions (Mark 7:13). By choosing tradition, the church has never been able to obtain anything God promised in the Bible. In America, the church don't seem to care about what God promises. They hold on to their traditions. So, I attended a revival. Although I had no interest in hearing the preachers, I was being supportive of the hosting pastors. Before I arrived at the service, the Lord talked to me about what to put in the offering plate that evening. It was a special seed to help this ministry meet its finances. When offering time came, one of the hosting pastors offended the congregation by telling them that he needed $20,000 by the end of the night to meet the budget. Then he said, <u>that God told him</u> that each leader present that night would give a specific amount. I don't remember the exact amount, but it was more than most of his own leaders would have been able to give. The Lord purposely told me what to give and my check was already written, but it was not in the amount the pastor was looking for. Then he asked for everyone who was giving that specific amount to bring the offering to the front of the church. No one got up. It was quite embarrassing because this huge church was packed, and yet nobody got up with an offering. That didn't stop the pastor from begging one more time. Again no one moved. He was about to ask a third time, when the Lord told me to get up and go down and take my offering to the front. Before I could get up, I had to repent. At first I was excited about giving, but when the pastor started pressuring people, my attitude changed. I was supposed to be sowing into that ministry to help their finances, but if I have ought against the pastor, my sowing would produce no harvest. I asked for forgiveness, and I asked the Lord to forgive the pastor because he truly did not know what he was doing.

When, I got up, the pastor said, "Finally, there's one obedient person in this church." As, he spoke it seemed that every eye was on me as I walked down the center aisle. Then the pastor said, what he should have said from the start, "If anybody has something to give, bring it now." This time, everyone got up and gave, but you could sense tension in the air. The Bible says that God loves a cheerful giver (II Corinthians 9:7), but sometimes church leaders make it difficult to do so. That particular pastor was desperate to meet his budget, but traditional offering tactics turn off congregations. That is why people believe that pastors are only interested in your money. It gives the church a bad reputation. I remember one offering experience that was hostile in nature, and I will never forget it. Two very well-known prophetesses were visiting this church. Again, I went to support the pastor. When it came time for the offering, the atmosphere immediately tensed up and the Holy Spirit said to me, **"Don't move until I tell you to."** This was a sign that something ugly was about to go down. Then one of the prophetess asked all ministry leaders to stand. I call this the traditional *Pentecostal shake down* method of taking up an offering. Then she demanded that we all give an amount she said <u>God told her that we should give</u>. No one moved. Then this woman went down by $50 increments and few if any moved. Anger was in her voice. When she got to $50, she began counting down by $10 increments, until she got to ten. Most everyone was still standing. This woman did the ultimate in intimidation tactics. She started at ten and said, "Doesn't anybody have $10 to give? Anybody?" Then she stared straight at me and counted down, "$9? 8? . . . $5?" When she got to $1, I was still standing in obedience to God. Then in total frustration, she said, "Does anybody have anything to give?" Then the Lord told me to move. It was also then that the entire congregation moved.

Now, the Bible is clear. *"Every man according as he purposeth in his heart, so let him give; not grudgingly, or of necessity: for God loveth a cheerful giver* (II Corinthians 9:7)." So, if God tells us to give as we desire in our hearts, why do pastors try to force you to give what they want you to give? If the Lord tells us to give, not grudgingly, why do leaders try to intimidate the congregation to give? It then becomes the case where the congregation is giving out of necessity; to keep from being publicly embarrassed. Therefore most givers become those who have ought in their hearts against the leader and ultimately against the church. These strong arm tactics are used to force large offerings out of the poorest people. These are the ones who desperately need to sow their way out of their poverty, but when they sow with a grudge, then their offering yields no fruit toward their deliverance, <u>unless</u> they repent before giving. Jesus said, *"Therefore if thou bring thy gift to the altar, and there rememberest that thy brother hath ought against thee; Leave there thy gift before the altar, and go thy way; first be reconciled to thy brother, and then come and offer thy gift* (Matthew 5:23-24)." Pastors and leaders need to be releasing the people from the bondage by letting them give freely so they can be blessed. Tradition says that leaders know best how to get money out of the people. They may get the money, but they also get the curse. The Kingdom is not trying to get money from people. God wants to get the Blessing to them. In order for that to happy, the people must obey and give as God tells them in their hearts, and they must give cheerfully.

These kind of pastors don't really care what happens to the people, they just want money to pay for the popular preachers they invited to speak. One pastor said from the pulpit, that he had asked another prophetess to speak, but she either wanted $20,000 up front, or all of the take from the offering plate. According to him, she refused to split the offering among the guest speakers. This is the Babylonian way of taking offerings in the church. It's about merchandising people and things for the money. Fortunately, not everyone does this, but there are enough that perform this way, to make it a strong tradition in the church. Jesus said, *"It is written, My house is the house of prayer: but ye have made it a den of thieves* (Luke 19:46).*"* Den of thieves indeed; not only in offerings, but also in merchandise. Don't believe me, check out the book tables. Years ago, the Lord gave me a dream in which he showed books and various Christian products displaying the faces of their authors. Until the Lord brought this to my attention, I had not noticed that this was a marketing technique used mainly for books by pastors and leaders of the church. The Lord said these people were using the name of Jesus to distribute their wares, based upon the popularity of the leader. The Lord called it **"spiritual junk food that will not feed the hungry soul, but will line the minister's pockets with cash."** According to the Lord, **"Their commercialism is causing the world to blaspheme the name of God."** The Lord then said that his people have heaped up for themselves leaders who entertain. Consequently, they are not equipped for the day of calamity, which is soon approaching. Thus says the Lord, **"These leaders have shut up the kingdom of heaven against men."**[2] They neither go in themselves, nor allow God's people to enter in (Matthew 23:13). Thank God for those prophetic writers who only publish what God tells them to produce. However, the majority of leaders have found a profitable way to merchandise their own name. With the Babylonian spirit, it's all about money and merchandising (Revelation 18:3).

---

2   Matthews Paula. "Year 2004: The Year of Completion, Journal Entry 10/31/04." *The War Journal (1999-2010) Volume I*. Los Angeles: Spirit & Life Publications[SM], 2010. 238. Print.

Finally, we want to briefly describe how the commandments and doctrine of men are also part of the Babylonian way of operating in the church. Volumes could be written on this alone. For it is the main area of difference amongst all Christians. It is also the area in which we are separated the furthest from the plan and purpose of God. Commandments are the rules that leaders impose upon men and women in the church, while doctrine are the teachings used to justify the commandments. The commandments of men are what men require of their congregations. They are usually something either unimportant to God or in direct opposition to what God says. Here is what concerns me about the commandments of men. They are <u>almost always</u> a hidden snare for their victims. Most times, these commandments are held in silence and are not spoken, until someone violates them. It can be quite startling to a new believer or to a new member of the church when they are embarrassed publicly for violated unspoken rules. These are often evil rules that place God's people in bondage to men. These commandments of men are almost always based upon flawed misinterpretations of Biblical scripture.

Some of the most obvious commands have to do with the role of women in the church and how they should dress. The only reason for such commandments is *sexual-phobia*. People call the church homo-phobic because of the general views about gays, but it's deeper than that. According to the Lord, the church is **"*wimpy and prudish"*** when it comes to sexual issues. Rather than strike these issues head-on with love and compassion, they make ungodly rules about men and women, and relationships. Again, whether held in silence or spoken over the pulpit, these commands have divided God's people universally, regardless of denomination. There are pastors who tell you, that they are just protecting the families from sexual sin, but a closer look shows that these wicked commands only cause people to become in bondage to fear. What manifests in their lives is the very thing that they fear. When you tell people not to do something, that is <u>the very thing</u> they will do. Consequently, the commandments and doctrines of men are largely ignored by those who are determined to sin.

On the surface, people appear to obey the rules, but behind closed doors they do what they want to do. Don't take my word for it, look around you. How many pastors and leaders have been found in adultery? How many others are in bondage to pornography and sexual perversion? Here is the problem with what is going on behind closed doors. It never stays behind closed doors. The church is a spiritual entity, and being so, even when it is in rebellion, Kingdom principles will always ring true. Jesus said it like this, *"For nothing is secret, that shall not be made manifest; neither any thing hid, that shall not be known and come abroad* (Luke 8:17)*."* Whatever is done in the dark, will eventually be exposed by the light. So, when women are forbidden to wear red lipstick or red nail polish it means nothing to those who really want to commit sin. Just because a woman wears red or wears makeup does not make her a Jezebel. Jezebel is a spirit of manipulation and control. It is a spirit that does not discriminate. Jezebel will operate through a man as well as a woman. Jezebel is a spirit of witchcraft. It has nothing to do with makeup, or the color red. Many times you will find that the real Jezebel is the one who is dresses and acts religious on the surface, but in their heart is a murderer and a fornicator.

If Christians are gravitating toward sin, it is a symptom of something more serious in the life of the believer. Perhaps it is fear, anger, hurt, or childhood or other trauma, from which they were never delivered. Too many leaders need deliverance, and instead of getting delivered, they place stringent rules on the people; even rules the leaders cannot perform. It's like the blind leading the blind. Both will fall into the ditch (Matthew 15:14). I heard one leader publicly commanded his pastors that if they were lusting after their secretaries, to fire her. Not knowing all the details, that sounded simply absurd. If the pastor is the one who is lusting, **he needs** deliverance. Firing the secretary will not cure him if lust is only in his heart. The Bible clearly tells us to flee fornication and adultery (I Corinthians 6:18). We are also told to abstain from all appearance of evil (I Thessalonians 5:22). Fleeing and abstaining connotes one's ability to remove and/or restrain <u>his or her own flesh</u>. Removing the person does not solve the problem, if it is done out of fear. It will only cause avoidance issues within the congregation, and may even cause the woman to leave the faith, if she did nothing wrong. This matter should be dealt with very delicately.

The pastor is the overseer; the father of the congregation. To lust after an employee or a congregant is spiritual incest. Jesus said that if a man has lusted after a woman, he has already committed adultery (Matthew 5:28). First and foremost, the sin of adultery must be eradicated. The leader in this example should have called such leaders to repent for having committed adultery in their hearts. Instead, he swept the issue under the carpet and told them to fire the women. Then there remains an adulterer as pastor, and that spirit which is upon him, will flow down to his leaders and then throughout the congregation (Numbers 11:24-25). This is a common issue in the church. There are leaders who are very popular with Christian audiences, but wherever they preach, adultery breaks out. It's a spirit they carry. No one ever pulled the preachers aside and told them to repent. Many should have been sat down and counseled, but instead, American congregations are ingesting their adulterous pollution. Consequently, fornication and adultery are common in the church. When Eli refused to chastise his sons for sleeping with the women in the church, God caused a curse to come upon the priest's entire family (I Samuel 2:22-36). Eli and his sons dishonored God. In one day, Eli and his entire house was destroyed as the Lord caused death to come upon them all (I Samuel 4:10-22).

Commandments of men cannot stop sin. They have no power over sin. Lust, like all sin is a cancer of the heart which can only be cured by the spirit. Commandments of men temporarily control the outward behavior, but out of the adulterous heart, the physical act of adultery will come to pass. It is that which is in the heart that defiles a man (Matthew 15:19-20). Eventually from the evil treasure of that heart, the person will commit adultery with his or her flesh (Matthew 12:35). Firing the secretary only delays the actual act of adultery if the pastor does not repent (change his mind and his behavior). What should be done? Instead of fleeing with his tail between his legs. The pastor needs to take dominion over the lust. The pastor should first submit himself to God in repentance and obey the instruction of the Holy Spirit for this situation. Then would he be sufficiently armed and capable to resist the devil. It is only under the authority of Almighty God that the lust devil will flee from him (James 4:7). Then, the devil will flee only for a season. He will try again, but if the pastors remains strong in faith and in his resolve to honor God, the devil will come, but he will not stay. Rules simply cannot prevent sin. How soon we forget how the Ten Commandments identified sin, but they did not deter men from sin. In fact, the opposite was true. That's the way of human nature. You who are in Christ, have yet another nature; one that is obedient to God. Obedience to God is not an option, it is a command. One has to yield to that godly nature, in order for it to operate in their lives. It is matter of choice.

Closely related to the issue of sex and fornication, is that of women preaching in the church. Men of God often want women in the back room praying, rather than in front of the congregation. They think it keeps men from lusting. They will even twist scripture to justify keeping women from obeying the call of God for their lives. They will often say that God did not call women to preach? The Bible tells of many women leaders appointed by God over his people. Deborah was a prophetess and judge over God's people (Judges 4:4). Esther was chosen as queen (Esther 2:16-17). Anna was a prophetess who was dedicated to serving God in the temple with fasting and prayer day and night (Luke 2:36-38). Dorcas was a noted disciple (Acts 9:36), as was Damaris (Acts 17:34).

God is no respecter of persons. He is a respecter of faith coming from a heart filled with love and obedience. Now, Jesus sent out the twelve (Matthew 10) and he sent out the seventy (Luke 10). We know the identity of the twelve, but we know nothing about the identity of the seventy nor do know all the identities of the one hundred twenty that were in the upper room (Acts 1:12-15). One thing we do know, there were women among them. Did early church only send men? It's very unlikely. They followed the pattern that Jesus left them. Jesus sent the woman at the well to go get her husband? She had none, but after realizing that Jesus was the Messiah, she dropped water pot and went back to Samaria. Because of her testimony, many believed on Jesus (John 4:1-42). He sent the mad man of the Gadarenes to his home and testify of the great things the Lord had done for him (Mark 5:18-20). It would seem that if Jesus sent these people out whom he met along the way, how much more would he have sent out the women who were a vital part of his ministry. Could **anyone** in the company of Jesus, watch the works of the Lord and not be compelled to preach the gospel? That is highly unlikely. Again, if Jesus did not call women to preach, why was it that after his resurrection, he chose to appear to the women first (Mark 16:1-13, John 20:11-18)? Women were the ones who preached the first message of the resurrection (Matthew 28:1-8). They preached it to the twelve and they did not believe (Luke 24:1-12). Each of the Gospel writers, confirm that the women were the first to see Jesus after the resurrection. He sent the women to the disciples with the good news. It does not make sense that the church would reject the notion of women preachers if they were clearly preaching during Jesus' day.

Even as I am writing, the Holy Spirit is reminding me of the woman with the alabaster box. Who poured the ointment on Jesus' feet and wiped his feet with her hair (Luke 7:36-50). Jesus said, *"Verily I say unto you, Wheresoever this gospel shall be preached in the whole world, there shall also this, that this woman hath done, be told for a memorial of her* (Matthew 26:13)*."* Women were always used mightily in preaching the Gospel message. There have always been women called to the five-fold ministry of apostles, prophets, evangelists, pastors and teachers (Ephesians 4:7-16). Some men are still saying that there are no apostles or prophets anymore. Others are denying the right of women to obey God's command to preach. This ought not be.

When the Lord said he was going to send me out like he did the first apostles. The pastors at my church heard God tell them to send me out, but they did nothing. One Sunday, I was invited to hear an apostle speak at another church. This man had been sent to Southeast Asia when Muslims were killing Christians at alarming rates. After his teaching, the apostle said that he had to obey God and send me out to do the work the Lord called me to do. Because of this one man's obedience, I was able to minister to pastors and leaders around the world. Who said that praying for the church was only a job for women? They obviously never paid attention to the Book of Acts. **The apostles were always in the word and in prayer daily** (Acts 1:14; 2:42; 4:31). When certain Grecians were complaining about their widows not being taken care of by the church, the twelve called the disciples and said, *"It is not reason that we should leave the word of God, and serve tables. Wherefore, brethren, look ye out among you seven men of honest report, full of the Holy Ghost and wisdom, whom we may appoint over this business. But we will give ourselves continually to prayer, and to the ministry of the word* (Acts 6:1-4)*."* The apostles spend most of their time in prayer and in the word. They didn't send the women in the back room to pray while they ran the church. The day-to-day business of the church was being done by the disciples, so that the apostles could continue daily in prayer and in the word. This was the pattern they learned from Jesus. *"When Jesus had spoken these words, he went forth with his disciples over the brook Cedron, where was a garden, into the which he entered, and his disciples. And Judas also, which betrayed him, knew the place: for Jesus ofttimes resorted thither with his disciples* (John 18:1-2; Matthew 26:36; Mark 14:32)*."* Jesus taught his disciples the importance of daily prayer. Never would he have told them to delegate prayer to the women amongst them while they did the work of the gospel. The struggle against women in the church began with many myths proliferated among men. Many bought the lie that says God cannot use women because Eve was deceived by the serpent in the Garden of Eden. They reason that since Eve was deceived, all women can easily be deceived as well, and should not be used of God in the church. Seriously? According to Genesis 3:6, when Eve was deceived, but Adam was not. He was standing there with her while the serpent beguiled her. Adam stood around and listened to the conversation between the serpent and his wife, and he did nothing. I believe that he used his wife to test God. While else would he watch and do nothing? Also, Eve told the serpent that God told them not to touch or eat the fruit (Genesis 3:3). If Eve was deceived, who set her up, Adam or the serpent, or both? Who told her that God said not to touch the fruit? God did not say this. Either Adam that told her, or she made it up. He got the original command directly from God. Eve was not there. She got the command second hand. If she was deceived by the serpent, it is also obvious that Eve was deceived by her husband as well. Why else would Adam be quick to accuse her? *"The woman whom thou gavest to be with me, she gave me of the tree, and I did eat (Genesis 3:12)."* Adam was quick to blame God and Eve, rather than taking responsibility for his own behavior. That is why God put the sin on Adam. He was the ruler who failed to rule over his subjects. This was Eli's problem. It is also the problem in the Babylonian church. Men are given headship, but they refuse to obey God because they are in bondage to their wives, to their children, to their congregations, to other men, and ultimately to their own flesh.

The Bible says, cursed is the man who departs from God and who is determined to do things by his own human efforts (Jeremiah 17:5). When men don't obey the command of God, a curse falls upon them and everything around them. They forfeit their dominion to that which they were commanded to dominate. Whatever we yield our members to obey, that becomes our master (Romans 6:16). Adam yielded to the serpent and the serpent became his master instead of God. We see the same in the church, when men decided to depart from God and follow another path. They no longer have the ability to take dominion over the evils of the earth. In fact, evil prevails in our world because God's men have departed from God to do their own thing. God does not blame the world for the evils it suffers. God blames the leaders of the church.

In Christ, we are all one Body, *"There is neither Jew nor Greek, there is neither bond nor free, there is <u>neither male nor female</u>: for ye are all one in Christ Jesus* (Galatians 3:28)." There is no difference between men and women in the Church Of Jesus Christ. We are all members of His Body. We are one in Christ. To deny women their rightful place in the church, is to deny the Body of Christ from functioning as one. Indeed that is exactly what has happened. The Body is trying to function with only select members, which leaves gaps and missing joints. Many parts are withering because they are not being amply supplied. Imagine what would happen in the human body, if you are missing an ankle. Your foot would be disconnected and the other leg would have to compensate for the lack of use of the disconnected one. Let's say that your knee was missing from the other leg. Then that leg is of no use in helping you get around. You would be crippled. When members are intentionally cut off from operating in the Body of Christ, it becomes spiritually crippled. It may look good on the outside, but it will not function as God intended. How could it function properly with parts missing? Here is a prophetic word. *"God has a plan for our dysfunction. Women of God, be of good cheer. The Lord is calling you up through the ranks. You had been relegated to praying in the back room. Therefore, many of you are more spiritually equipped then the men are to take on the spiritual darkness that is coming upon the earth. God is about to use you mightily. The Lord also reminded me of several prophecies he had given me about the end-time wealth transfer. The wealth will be coming to the "prayer warriors," those who fought the battles on their knees. When the men sent the women into the back rooms to pray, it was meant to be condescending, but the Lord had another plan. While they were busy following men, you were following God. You have done what Jesus and the first apostles did. You went up to the mountain in prayer all night, and you will come down walking in miraculous power. When all is said and done, you will walk away with the spoils. Take heed. In these last days, whoever has the money and knows how to pray, will hold all the Kingdom power. Women of God, what the devil meant for evil, God will turn for his glory. He will bring you forth with silver and gold (Psalm 105:37)! Hallelujah!"*

Here is another note for the men and women of God. I want to mention something that the Lord has had me sharing with pastors and their wives over the years. This is especially for those in prophetic ministries. God sees you and your spouse as **one body**, just as Jesus and the church are one body. In the church, the Spirit of God will use the gifts *as the spirit wills*. The same will be true in your family. You may be the spiritual head and may be even a pastor, but if God called you, the message he wants to speak may be given to your spouse to speak instead. It may even be given to one of your offspring. The first time the Lord gave me this word, one pastor was in shock and even offended. In his church, women were not permitted to speak, not even his wife. Once the pastor yielded to what the Lord had to say, the Lord had me lay hands on the entire family so that the spirit could have freedom to move in that church. Every member of that family had speaking gifts, some prophesied, some taught and others sang. Again, God is not respecter of person. He is a respecter of faith. We must give God the freedom to move.

Religion, tradition, commandments of men are truly an unholy alliance against the Kingdom of God. Instead of preaching and demonstrating the power of the gospel, this unholy trinity is causing members of the Body to commit treason against the Kingdom. Instead of believing the truth about Jesus, they are fostering and promoting hypocrisy and lies that the Body had adopted as truth. Instead of saving souls and training a powerful supernatural army, the church is majoring on minor things such as whether women should wear pants or makeup, or whether people should smoke or drink. And, who said that all gay people go to hell? This is a lie. People are being taught that these are the things that will send them to hell. This is a shameful mockery of the Blood of Jesus. No one has ever gone to hell just because of these things. So, what is it that sends people to hell? It's not **what** people do that sends them to hell. It's **who** they reject that sends them to hell. Jesus is the only way to God (John 14:6). He is **The Door**. Enter by this door and you shall be saved. He is the good shepherd who came that we might have life and that we mighty have it more abundantly (John 10:9-10). All that matters to God is whether you go through **The Door**. Did you receive Jesus? You can go through **The Door** smoking, drinking, wearing pants and being gay. This is a *door of transformation* for whomsoever would believe what Jesus says. Walk through **that** door and the Holy Spirit will do the work. Jesus said that is was better to enter into life maimed, than to have two hands be cast into hell, in the fire that never shall be quenched: where their worm dies not and the fire is not quenched (Mark 9:43-44). If you offend someone who received Jesus, regardless of their imperfections, Jesus said it would better for you that a millstone were hanged about your neck and you were cast into the sea (Mark 9:42). What then? Do we allow sin to prevail in our lives? God forbid. We must understand that God is calling all men to come to his son to receive life. **They must come as they are**, not when they are perfected. Perfection is a supernatural act that can only be performed by the Holy Spirit. It is not done by obeying the rules of men. In fact, the American Church looks a lot like that of the Jews of Jesus' day. They were preoccupied with the tradition of washing of cups, pots and tables, but they never considered cleaning the inside of their hearts. They honored God with their lips, but their hearts are far from him (Mark 7:1-6). They worshiped God in vain because they set aside the commandments of God in order to teach the doctrines and commandments of men. In short, they preferred their religious ways rather than God's way. The same is true of the church today.

One of the most evil doctrines being taught is that which says that the Holy Spirit is not available, nor is he necessary in our day. They take it even further by teaching that tongues and the gifts of the spirit have ceased operating. Some believe that we have evolved past the time of needing the Holy Spirit and his gifts. We have technology. So, what do they think about those who are operating by the spirit, and who are manifesting the gifts? They call them false prophets, which is quite bizarre when you think about it. Those who are <u>not demonstrating</u> the power of Jesus call themselves true believers, but they call <u>those who are walking like Jesus,</u> are called the false believers. That shows just how far the American church has fallen away from God. This is how the Babylonian spirit works. It convinces men that their way is right even though it opposes what God has said in his word.

So, What is the truth, about the Holy Spirit and the gifts of the spirit? Has technology replaced the need for the Holy Spirit as some preach? God forbid! Is technology the Spirit of Truth? Does it guide us into all truth? Does technology hear the things of God and show us things to come (John 16:13)? Is technology the third person of the Godhead? It would be odd to even hear someone say, "I bless you in the name of the Father, and the son, and the holy technology." Did Jesus or the apostles cast out demons or heal the sick using technology? Did Jesus use technology to multiply the fish and the loaves to feed the five thousand? Did technology help Jesus walk on the water or help him calm the raging seas? Did technology raise Jesus from the dead? Is that same technology residing within the heart of every believer quickening our mortal bodies to do the will of the father (Romans 8:11)? Then, it should be obvious that if Jesus needed the Holy Spirit in order to carry out the Father's will, we need him too. In fact, we cannot even begin to do what Jesus did without the Holy Spirit. That is why he told the apostles that they would receive power after the Holy Ghost had come (Acts 1:8). Well, folks the Holy Ghost has been here ever since, and he will reside with us forever (John 14:16-17). Jesus said that those who believe in him would do the works that he did and would do even greater works because he goes to the father (John 14:12).

Religious people will continue to hold the truth in unrighteousness. They know the truth, yet they refuse to recognize it as the truth. To recognize the truth means that they have to come clean with their hypocrisy. For that to happen would require an act of God. Even then, many would never recognized God if he showed up. They didn't recognize Jesus. They still don't. Therefore, religious people will continue in worthless commands and doctrine that send people through self-righteousness, but God's righteousness **will never** be obtained that way. The Holy Spirit is the only one who can lead us to the path of righteousness and keep us there. Without the supernatural "keeping" power of the Holy Ghost, power of God is nullified and Christianity is reduced to a set of rules. It's not that God and his word are not working. It's that the Holy Spirit is not allowed his place in most Christian lives. Jesus said he sent the Spirit of Truth that would guide us to all the truth; that he would show us things to come (John 16:13). Preachers say that we have technology; that is the only truth we need, but that is not what Jesus said. **Jesus say that he was the Truth** (John 14:6)? How then, can holy men say that technology is truth? Therein lies the core of all issues of the Babylonian church in America. They refuse to acknowledge that God's word is truth. Consequently, the people of God are no longer seeking the truth. They are not seeking Jesus. The church will never know its purpose In Christ, until it knows Jesus Christ. Who was he? Why was he sent? What has this to do with me? Christians in America are not asking these questions. They are not seeking the face of God for answers, because they think they already know the truth. Religion is a facade; a fig leaf in which man uses to cover his own nakedness cause by sin. These are those who mock the Blood Jesus and make the word of God of no effect. It becomes null and void in their lives. Here is the real danger of religion. Anyone who would pervert the truth of God, will pervert the truth about marriage and about life in general. These are vile persons who have exchanged the truth of God for the lie (Romans 1:24-25)

When the Lord gave me that vision of the American church and call it an organization built *"in the similitude of the Tower of Babel,"* that was indeed an accurate assessment of what's wrong in America; not just the church, but also the government, our education system and our business philosophy. No one wants to know the truth. The church openly condemns and curses the worldly aspects of America, not realizing that the country is simply reacting to the lack of spiritual authority. Without the Holy Spirit, the church has no authority. Why condemn America when it is the church who is at fault? If we want to change America, it begins with restoring the church to its original Kingdom purpose. Religion makes a mockery of the cross and renders the Blood of Jesus powerless. According to the Lord, rejecting the seed of his word (the truth) makes his people *"abortionists."* Here is the revelation the Holy Spirit gave me. *"The Lord continued to say that there are many more abortionists within the church than outside the church. These are those that took God's spiritual seed and killed it. Because a life was taken, one will also be required in the spirit if Christians do not repent. Jesus said He would cast out those He never knew (Matthew 7:21-23). God's people intentionally choose their own way and abort God's. This is a more prevalent and serious offense against God. He said that the world is expected to kill babies. They don't know God. The church is called to know God, yet has the boldness to kill His spiritual babies and keep those fathered by Satan."*[3]

With God, there is only black or white. You are either for him or against him. There is no gray area. Jesus told the church at Laodicea that he wished they were either hot or cold, but since they were lukewarm, he would spew them out of his mouth. This was a church that had money and thought it had it all together. Jesus called them to repent. He even said that he was standing at the door of their hearts knocking; waiting for them to open to him so he can commune with them. To those who repent (overcome), the Lord offers to sit at his throne, just like Jesus overcame this world and now sits at his father's throne. Let him that has ears to hear, let him hear what the Spirit is saying to the churches (Revelation 3:14-22).

---

[3] Matthews, Paula. "Year 2004: The Year Of Completion Journal Entry 10/28/04 Abortion—The Death of God's Seed.". *The War Journal (1999-2010) Volume I*. Los Angeles: Spirit & Life Publications, 2010.237. Print.

The Hidden Gospel Of The Kingdom

One of the reasons that the Spirit of Babylon is such a force in the American Church has to do with how the gospel message has been interpreted and taught over the past several hundred years. We discussed the some of those misinterpretations of scriptures in the previous chapter. In this chapter we will see how God intentionally shrouded the gospel of his Kingdom in mysteries that have been hidden since the foundation of the world. God never reveals his entire plan to humans. He unveils kingdom mysteries according to our faith, and then he only reveals to us as we move from one level of faith to another level of faith. It's almost like graduating and being promoted from one class level to the other. The problem with most Christians is that they stopped getting promoted around the kindergarten or first grade level of the spirit. Therefore they have virtually no knowledge of the Kingdom, except to know that it exists. Where it exists and how it functions, never entered into their learning. Many think that God's way is too hard to learn, so they just drop out and let their pastors and other men of God tell them what to believe. In a perfect world, this would be somewhat of a positive thing, but most leaders of the church have been taught erroneous doctrine. They have no knowledge of the truth about God's Kingdom.

In all my years of working with pastors, the greatest hurdle was getting over how, and what, they had been taught by their own leaders. Most were trained to teach about heaven and hell, but virtually nothing was ever taught about God's Kingdom. The Lord sent me to teach the mysteries of the Kingdom. They had been taught that everything centered around the church, but the church is only a portion of the Kingdom. They know how to prepare sermons and perform administrative duties, but have no knowledge about ministering to their own spiritual needs. They were therefore, not equipped to minister to the need of their congregations. Many leaders run in packs, where one leader tells the others how to operate. This rarely included prayer, fasting and researching the word concerning the mysteries of the Kingdom. They had thrown out the supernatural power of the gospel for the wisdom of men. The gospel is hidden to the majority of the Body of Christ in America because no one is actively pursuing God and his will. Babylon seeks its own will. Unfortunately that means that the church is not currently equipped to handled the tribulation of these last days. Indeed, the church **will be here** for the tribulation. The Lord told me to prepare the leaders for severe persecution during these end-times. We won't be able to survive without the supernatural in these days. First and foremost, God's people need to unlock the mystery of God's will for the earth. We covered that earlier in this book. We discovered that God's original purpose was to give humans this earth as an inheritance, to manage as God manages in heaven. It wasn't until Jesus resurrected, that there have been humans equipped to take back what Satan stole from Adam, and to recapture our inheritance. These are the people of God, the church. The problem is, the church at large, has virtually no idea of who they are and why they are in existence. They know what learned men have told them, but they have virtually no revelation from heaven concerning the matter. If the gospel is hidden, it is only hidden to those who are lost. Indeed in the church as we know it in America is lost, but <u>all is not lost</u>. The Apostle Paul prayed one of the most powerful prayers for the church, *"That the God of our Lord Jesus Christ, the Father of glory, may give unto you the spirit of wisdom and revelation in the knowledge of him* (Ephesians 1:17).*"* Paul's greatest desire is for the church to be given the spirit of wisdom and revelation in the knowledge of God. If the church is to survive, it is vital that they be revived with wisdom from God. They have chosen the wisdom of men and the wisdom of this world, but *to arise to their calling*, the church has to desire wisdom from above. That means going back to the serious study of the word and earnest prayer. It means allowing the Holy Spirit, and not men to interpret the word of God for their lives and ministries.

In addition, the church needs a true revelation in the knowledge of God; who he is, and what his plan is for the world and for their calling (Ephesians 1:18). If you don't know God or his purpose for your life, how do you proceed? In the past the church has relied on what men have done in the past. This worked for a short season, but God is ever increasing. He is not stagnant. If we want what he has for this season, we have to do things the Kingdom way. These are the last days, the only thing that will survive, are those things built upon God's Kingdom principles and purpose. These are the only things that will not be shaken in these last days. We must go to God for his wisdom and revelation for last days survival. Each member of the Body has been given a last day's assignment, that comes only from spending quality time with the Father, otherwise, it won't be known. Too often the American Church treats God as if he is on some far away planet zillions of miles from the earth. If you are a member of the Body, the Holy Spirit (the third person of the Godhead) dwells in you. If you are the temple of God's Spirit, then you are only a prayer away from God and his will. It won't just drop out of the sky. You have to go after it like *great treasure* (Matthew 13:44). That is another problem in the American Church, they don't value God, or Jesus as their Lord. They confess him with their mouths, but in practice, God's people have chosen to be lord over their own lives. Remember that the prophecy the Lord gave me showed the American Church as having no head. It's members are in agreement that it needs no head, but in these last days, the headless church will not stand. This is not the church that Jesus built. If Jesus is not their Lord, then Satan is automatically the lord over their lives. I know some have been taught that there is God, the devil and us. That is not true. Jesus said it himself, if you are not with him, you are against him (Luke 11:23). Are you shocked? You shouldn't be. Take a look at Adam. When he chose to do his own thing rather than following God, who took over his life? Was it Adam or was it Satan? Still not convinced, let's look at scripture. The Bible says that whoever you yield your members (body) to obey, becomes your master (Romans 6:16); whether to sin and death or to obedience and righteousness. It's simple, if you want what God promises, you have to yield your members to obey God. In our day, we rarely see the glory of God because men are too distracted to obey God.

Consider this. The Gospels of Matthews, Mark, Luke and John tell the story of how Jesus came to preach the gospel of the kingdom to the poor. Whether lacking money, or they were brokenhearted, physically and spiritually blind or captive, Jesus was anointed with the Holy Ghost and power. He went about doing good and healing all who were oppressed by the devil (Acts 10:38). The gospel was demonstrated not only in words, but also in supernatural deeds. After his resurrection, Jesus appeared to many witnesses including his apostles. He commanded that they be endued with the Holy Spirit and then go be a witness of his resurrection and the power of his Kingdom over death, and over all the power of the enemy that is keeping people in bondage. The church was based upon this witness and this message. It was supposed to be passed to the nations of the earth and passed from generation to generation until the entire earth was filled with the glory like it was in Adam's day. There is so much lack and suffering in our world, why isn't the church taking dominion? Why isn't the church preaching the real gospel today?

The things of God and his Kingdom are often shrouded in mystery. To a wise man it is a pleasure to seek out these mysteries, but to those whose hearts are evil toward God they remain a mystery. Often this mysteriousness of God inflames evil hearts to disobedience. The truth is before them, but if they want to know it, they have go to God. This they refuse to do. Why does God hide his precious things in a mystery? Some believe he is playing games and wants to do us harm. This is what the serpent wanted Adam and Eve to think. The devil knew this line of thought would cause them to rebel against God. Just because there are mysteries surrounding the things of God, does not mean that God is withholding things to harm us. He is a good God. He loves us and would only give us his best. Here is what King Solomon had to say about the mysteries of God. *"It is the glory of God to conceal a thing: but the honour of kings is to search out a matter* (Proverbs 25:2).*"*

It pleases God when we pursue him and his word. That is why he rewards those who diligently seek him (Hebrews 11:6). Here is the good news. Those secret things of God are hidden as a treasure for God's children. *"The secret things belong unto the LORD our God: but those things which are revealed belong unto us and to our children for ever* (Deuteronomy 29:29).*"* God reveals his secrets to his children so that they can perform what is necessary to bring forth His treasures in the earth. Someone has to hear the words of God and believe what he is saying, then do what is required to obtain that great treasure. But again, the sinful nature of man causes mens' hearts to be blinded. They cannot see nor can they hear what God is saying. The words of God are incomprehensible to fallen man. His language is confusing to them, just as confusing as it was when God disrupted those who wanted to erect the Tower of Babel. In Babel, once their languages were confused, they didn't try to bridge that communication gap. They just went their separate ways to obey God. A similar, yet opposite thing happens when God's word is spoken before evil and wicked men. They don't even try to understand what God is saying. They simply dismiss it as nonsense, and continue doing evil. For this reason, Jesus came to earth speaking in parables to the ancient Jews. Even Jesus' disciples wondered by he never spoke plainly to everyone. *"And the disciples came, and said unto him, Why speakest thou unto them in parables? He answered and said unto them, Because it is given unto you to know the mysteries of the kingdom of heaven, but to them it is not given. For whosoever hath, to him shall be given, and he shall have more abundance: but whosoever hath not, from him shall be taken away even that he hath* (Matthew 13:10-12)." Jesus was telling the *Parable Of The Sower*, when his disciples asked him this question. This parable, as Jesus later explains, tells of how the condition of a person's heart will determined if they can hear and bring forth fruit for God's Kingdom. Those who **have** a receptive heart, will freely receive even more in abundance; but to those who **have not** a receptive heart, that which they hear will be taken from them. They will receive nothing from the Kingdom. That is why Jesus often said, *"He that hath ears to hear, let him hear."* We all have ears on the side of our heads, but the ears he is talking about has to do with our hearts. Can you hear with your heart? Is there a connection between you and God in which you are able to catch the nuances and dark speech, and let it illuminate your heart? That is a gift that God gives to those who love him. Those who love him, are those who are willing to obey him. So, when they hear, they don't just listen with their ears. They listen with an intent to obey what they hear. This is the kind of heart that **has receptivity** and it will bring forth what God is promising. These are those who have ears to hear.

If the heart is the receptacle that God uses, then it has to be cleansed and purified in order to receive the word of the Kingdom. People can often fool other people, because they are looking at outer appearances. God, on the other hand, looks at a person's heart (I Samuel 16:7). Are they listening attentively, or are they distracted with other things? Are they speaking in honesty, or are they saying what others want to hear? Are they plotting and scheming against others? Are they holding unforgiveness against another? If the heart is in anyway defiled, it cannot receive anything from God's Kingdom. Instead, they will bring forth the evil things that have been allowed to defile their hearts. From out of the evil treasure of an evil man's heart, he will bring forth evil (Matthew 12:35). How do we know what is inside the heart of a man? Listen to how he speaks. For out of the abundance of the heart, his mouth will speak (Matthew 12:34). These are the evils that defile a man. *"But those things which proceed out of the mouth come forth from the heart; and they defile the man. For out of the heart proceed evil thoughts, murders, adulteries, fornications, thefts, false witness, blasphemies: These are the things which defile a man: but to eat with unwashen hands defileth not a man* (Matthew 15:18-20)." How does one purify his own heart? Jesus said it this way, *"Sanctify them through thy truth: thy word is truth* (John 17:17)." We are cleansed by the washing of the water of the word

(Ephesians 5:26). It was the word we first received at salvation that began the process, but that was not the end of the cleansing process. Unfortunately, this is often where most Christians stop. They got cleaned up just enough to get into heaven, but let me share what the Lord gave me many years ago about the cleansing process. It is a personal story that opened my eyes to how God purposed our salvation.

I was visiting a friend of mine in the Midwest. She offered me something to drink while we were standing around in her dimly lit kitchen. My friend took a glass out of the dishwasher, and from my vantage point, there was a large lipstick print on the rim of the glass. I thought my friend saw it too, until she began to pour me a drink in that glass. I told her that the glass was not clean. My friend told me it had to be clean because it just went through a cycle in the dishwasher. Rather than argue with her, I just switched on the overhead lights in the kitchen and then she saw it. My friend was quite embarrassed because she was about to argue with me about the cleanliness of the glass. The Lord used that example to show me how his people think. Most Christians think that because they have spoken the prayer of salvation that they are totally clean. No! That was just the beginning of the process. The cleansing process is a continual process as we grow in the things of God. That is why we must renew our minds (Romans 12:2) by continuing to hear and obey the word. It is not just the hearing, but the hearing and obeying the word that cleanses us.

Even if we cleanse our hearts from these things, we must always have eyes to see and ears to hear what God is saying to us. Remember that the Kingdom of God is within us. It is the treasure that has been deposited into the heart of every believer. The Holy Spirit put it there, but it is up to us to search for it and release that treasure upon the earth. Your heart is where the treasure is buried, but it takes the Holy Spirit and your cooperation with Him to bring it to pass. It begins with properly tuning your ears to hear the voice of the Spirit. That means blocking out all distractions and giving the Lord one hundred percent of your attention. Life has many distractions and the enemy is sure to send things to divert attention away from God. Even simple things like being over worked or over tired can affect how you hear. Believe it or not, what you eat and when you eat can also affect how you hear. This is something the Lord taught me years ago. Most of what I have learned and what I teach, came directly from the Holy Spirit. I went through a *Holy Ghost Boot*

Camp. He taught me how to intercede for God's people, but it was the most unusual training. The Spirit of God would descend upon me and arrest my spirit. At least that is what it felt like. The Holy Spirit would show up and my spirit would take off while I was praying in tongues. When I say take off, that is truly what happened. I would be praying for someone in China, and the next moment I would actually be there physically rescuing someone. This was no ordinary intercession. I was flying around to various locations in the world while praying for the nations.

I learned obedience through what I suffered. When the Lord told me to seek his face, many years ago, that is exactly what I did. I sought him with my whole heart, and when I found him. I asked why it was that he kept beckoning me by saying, **"Seek My Face."** I had been praying up to that point. I knew his voice. I was obeying him, to the best of my ability, but there was even more in store for my life. The mysteries of the Kingdom were slowly unfolding before my face. This was before I was filled with the Holy Spirit. I had visions and dreams and I often took off in the spirit while having discussion with the Lord. After I was spirit-filled, things went into another dimension. The Lord began revealing more of his Kingdom and how it operated. I asked the Lord, "How close do you want me to seek you?" He responded, **"How close do you want to be?"** Like a little child, I said, "I don't want any distance between us." Since that day, the Lord has been pouring out of his Spirit into my spirit. The things I have learned could have never been discovered in this physical realm. Only God could share what I have learn about His hidden Kingdom. Which brings us to the next questions: Why is the Kingdom hidden? We know that it is the glory of God to conceal a matter, but why does he do it? Why did God choose to hide his Kingdom? When I first asked the Lord this question, he reminded me of how His glory left the earth after Adam sinned. There was no way to return the glory in all its fullness except for completely destroying earth and all creation, and starting over again. Instead, God said he chose to place His glory (the Kingdom) inside the hearts of obedient men. He called it the **"treasure in earthen vessels,"** which is *"Christ in you, the hope of glory"* (Colossians 1:27). *"[1]* Now, the glory of the Kingdom is revealed from faith to faith in the lives of obedient believers. The more obedient we are, the more glory that is revealed in the earth. Christians often think that God's glory will come out of the sky, when in actuality, the glory is

---

1   Matthews, Paula. "Author's Note On Seeking Great Treasure."*Seeking And Enjoying The True Treasure Of This Life.*" Shaker Heights: Spirit & Life Publications[SM], 2013. 15. Print.

within us. We release God's glory in the earth through our obedience. It comes from within us and comes upon us. People are waiting for God to pour out his spirit, and he is waiting for us to obey him.

Recently I was singing a praise song with a congregation. The words of the song were telling God to pour out his spirit. When I first began to sing, there was a strange feeling inside of me. The Lord said, *"I have poured out my spirit. He's already here!"* I immediately shut my mouth and could not sing another word of that song. The Lord reminded me of what happened when he poured out his spirit after Jesus resurrected and they all began speaking in tongues (Acts 2:14-21). From there the Lord reminded me that we are now at <u>the end</u> **of the last days**, and the church has done nothing. He gave us his word, his son, the Holy Spirit and the grace to get the job done, but the American Church has chosen to do its own thing. Even those who know the plan of God are choosing to do it in their own strength and power. They are not following the instructions of God. Instead, they are taking the advice of men who went before them. These men are expecting God to do things the way he has always done them. Consequently, the church thinks the worst is over. They are expecting Jesus to come any day to take the church out of here. According to the Lord, they will be greatly disappointed because the church will not exit the earth until after the tribulation (Matthew 24:29-30; Mark 13:26). They have chosen to disconnect themselves from God and connect only to men. The church has little to no knowledge of what it is to come upon the earth. Like Babel, they have built a tower to promote themselves, but God is about to scatter them all.

The gospel may be hidden, but only to those who are lost (II Corinthians 4:3). The church as we know it is indeed lost. In their rebellion against the plan of God, the enemy has blinded their hearts and minds to the truth, but there is about to be a serious wake up call in America. Unfortunately, when the tribulation begins, many will fall away from the faith because they will not be able to handle the pressure of these last days. The church has no idea of the great treasure God has placed inside each of us. Jesus gave us the same glory that the father gave him (John 17:22) We also have the fullness of Christ inside of us waiting to be released (John 1:16). Here is a glimpse of what God has placed inside us. *"The key thing to remember about God's mysteries, and all of the kingdom, is that it all begins and ends at the cross. In that one simple act of hearing and receiving, the power of God thru the Holy Spirit comes into our lives and delivers us out of the kingdom of darkness and translates us into the kingdom of God's dear son (Colossians 1:13). This is all made possible because of what Jesus did on the cross. "The Cross of Jesus Christ is a sign of God's, covenant just the like rainbow was a sign of God's covenant in Noah's day, and circumcision was a sign of the covenant in the days of Moses. The blood covenant is alive and active today. The Lord called the cross "a portal into God's Kingdom that has the ability to impart both the power and wisdom of God to transform any and every situation on this earth." Preachers preach the cross and sin, but very few talk about the transforming power behind the cross; which is the power of the Holy Spirit. This is the same power that raised Jesus from the dead, and it is made available to every believer today. "The Holy Spirit searches the deep things of God and reveals them to our spirits. This is the glory of God placed within men. Here is how the Holy Spirit explained it to me. "The script for our lives is revealed to our hearts by the spirit; in the form of a vision; a dream; a spoken word or a "knowing." The vision or dream from God is activated by our faith. Our tongue is the ready writer that brings it to pass; just like it was when God spoke and brought all of creation to pass." At creation, the Spirit of the Lord hovered over the deep. He was waiting for God's word to be spoken so that he could bring it to pass. God saw darkness and commanded light to be. Light came into existence. God saw lack, void and disorder in the earth and called forth from his spirit all of creation as we know it today. Because of the completed work of Jesus Christ on the cross, this same creative power is available inside every believer. "The completed work on the cross gives us the access to God's secrets and the power to create what God desires in this earth. Without activating this covenant connection we could do nothing in the kingdom."[2]*

God gave us dominion and everything we need to restore about his glory in the earth, but it can only manifest when we speak God's words and obey his instructions. This is where Babylon takes a detour. The church speaks its own words of agreement with other men. God is not in the picture. Oh, they may mention his name. They may even end their prayers saying, "in Jesus' name," but their hearts are far away from him. The tower is the center of Babylon's universe, and so it is with the church. In many ways the American Church is a carbon copy of the ancient Jews who rejected the Messiah to do their own thing. They are

---

2   Matthews, Paula."Releasing The Glory Within." *The Glory Of God Revealed Through The Lives Of Ordinary Men.* Shaker Heights: Spirit & Life Publications[SM], 2014. 43. Print.

still waiting for the Messiah to show up and he has already been here. Likewise, the church is waiting for an outpouring and the glory to show up, but it is already here. It is in the Kingdom inside of us. It was never hidden. It's been inside the spirit of every born again believer all the time. This is our treasure. Instead of treasuring what God gave us, most Christians are treasuring the Jews. This is taking a huge step backwards. Some also teach that the final judgment will be about the Jews and not about Jesus Christ at all. What does the Bible say? Here is a quote from the Apostle Paul, *"For we must all appear before the judgment seat of Christ; that every one may receive the things done in his body, according to that he hath done, whether it be good or bad* (II Corinthians 5:10)." *"In the day when <u>God shall judge the secrets of men by Jesus Christ</u> according to my gospel* (Romans 2:16)." *"And the times of this ignorance God winked at; but now commandeth all men every where to repent: Because he hath appointed a day, in the which he will judge the world in righteousness by that man whom he hath ordained; whereof he hath given assurance unto all men, in that he hath raised him from the dead* (Acts 17:30-31)."

Here is the amazing thing. God did not reveal <u>this</u> treasure to the religious Jews of his day. He revealed it through his holy apostles and prophets to the church. He continues to unveil his treasure through his church. This *Hidden Kingdom* (God's glory) remained hidden in a mystery until after Jesus' resurrection. It wasn't even revealed to all the apostles immediately. After his conversion, Apostle Paul was called to take the message to the Gentiles (Ephesians 3:8-11). Understand that Jesus and the first apostles were Jews. After the resurrection, Jesus ordained the church to take the message of the gospel to the world. The message was first given to the Jews, but then went to the world. So, the church was made up of Jews and Gentiles who were converted to Christianity. According to the Blood Covenant of Jesus Christ, you had to be born again to be an son and heir of God. Therefore the secrets and the inheritance was made available to only those who received Jesus as Lord. The religious Jews of that day rejected Jesus and the message of the kingdom. Therefore they were not eligible to receive the inheritance, which is for those who have faith in Jesus. *"For as many as are led by the Spirit of God, they are the sons of God. For ye have not received the spirit of bondage again to fear; but ye have received the Spirit of adoption, whereby we cry, Abba, Father. The Spirit itself beareth witness with our spirit, that we are the children of God: And if children, then heirs; heirs of God, and joint-heirs with Christ* (Romans 8:14-17)." Every human on earth has the potential to be an heir of God, but they have to come to Jesus Christ first. There are people in the church, but they are not in Christ. They visit, but they have never joined the family. God's secret treasure is reserved for his family. The Jews as a whole, have some knowledge of God's secrets, but until they recognize Jesus as their Messiah, they will not have the same access that has been granted to the church. Now, God is sovereign. He can appear to anyone, at anytime and call them into his family. I know of several cases where that has happened. In fact, I have come to believe that wherever God sends me, that he will touch the lives of those who don't know him.

Once, the Lord sent me on an hour drive to meet someone. I knew it was urgent, but he gave me no details other than ***"Go!"*** When I arrived at the building the Lord led me to, a woman grabbed me from behind saying, "You're the one he sent." The woman shared how she was visited by Jesus Christ who said he had called her to be a prophet to her nation. The woman was a Jew. She said she didn't even believe in Jesus and yet he appeared to her. According to this woman, the Lord took her to a grave yard and told her to open her mouth. When she did, the dead arose from their graves. He gave her a message for the Jewish people. She shared the message with her parents, who shared it with the Rabbi. They labeled her an heretic. When I met her, she was contemplating suicide because she couldn't handle the pressure. In her desperation, this Jewish woman told the Lord to confirm his call by sending someone to her. The Lord sent me to minister to her. Fortunately, I knew of similar cases with other Non-Christians. This gave her some peace. The Lord had me exhort her to speak his word exactly like she heard it and leave the results to him. I laid hands on her, prayed and sent her out to fulfill what God called her to do.

Then, there was the young Persian woman I knew on a casual basis. I never knew her last name, but God knew her. One night while sleeping, the Lord called out her first and last name. I immediately sat up in bed and began praying for her. The next morning the woman came to my office to see me. Whenever I had seen her in the past, it was about business, nothing spiritual, but this particular day was different. She walked up to me and said, "The man upstairs told me that I should talk to you about a dream I had last night." Now, this Persian woman and I had a very friendly and sometimes playful relationship, so I replied, "The man upstairs. Oh, you mean the man in room #__ in your apartment building." I don't remember what room number I mentioned, but she leaned over my desk, pointed upwards and responded, "You know, . . . the man upstairs." Then she told me about her frightening dream. She said that in this dream, she and her mother were attempting to escape from their apartment building that had been bombed along with many other buildings. "They were my people, who did the bombing." She knew that they were Persians, whether from America or from Iran, this woman knew for sure that they were her people. Evidently, she cried out to God after that dream and the Lord showed up and told her to pray for her people and for Iran. As a Muslim, she did not understand why someone other than Allah had answered her call, but she knew it was real. She just didn't know what to call him, so she called him *the man upstairs*. I confirmed that her dream was accurate, but that God needed us to intercede by praying for divine intervention in that situation. When she realized that it was Jesus, she was more than impressed with a God that loved people and wanted to protect them. This young woman asked me to pray for her because she and her mother were heading to Teheran for a few weeks. Her mother wanted to visit her family there. The Lord gave this young Persian woman instructions to pray during her stay in Iran. This was an official assignment for the Kingdom of God and the woman didn't know who called her, but she accepted the call. The woman returned with a good report. She prayed like God told her to and there were no incidents during her travels.

The more the Lord sends me to the different people of the world, the more I realize that it is sometimes easier for Him to reach the nonbeliever who is seeking God, than to reach the believer who is not seeking God. Jesus told the Jews of this day that the Kingdom was within (Luke 17:20-21), but they had no ears to hear, so he never revealed any more. The same has happened with the American Church. Not only have they ceased seeking God, many still believe that God does not speak to men today. Their religion and tradition have disqualified them from obtaining their inheritance. So they continue living their lives like orphans having no future and no hope. They talk about what God will do, but somehow he never quite does it for them. They bear no fruit that God is who he says he is. They are disenfranchised Christians who don't know who they are. We should keep them lifted in prayer with the prayer Paul prayed for the Ephesians, *"That the eyes of your(their) understanding being enlightened; that ye (they) may know what is the hope of his call-*

ing, and what the riches of the glory of his inheritance in the saints, (Ephesians 1:18)." God is desperately looking for anyone who will hear his voice and obey him. Earlier we said that he rewards those who diligently seek him (Hebrews 11:6). We also know from scripture that, *"The eyes of the LORD run to and fro throughout the whole earth, to shew himself strong in the behalf of them whose heart is perfect toward him* (II Chronicles 16:9)." Even if they never knew him before, God will reveal himself to those who have an ear to hear. Once he has their ear, he will identify who they are in his eyes. The Jewish woman was called as prophet and the Lord demonstrated the power he placed within her. The Persian woman was called to be his intercessor for her nation. They were blessed to have heard, and God blessed them even more for their obedience. Isn't that what the Bible says would happen? *"Eye hath not seen, nor ear heard, neither have entered into the heart of man, the things which God hath prepared for them that love him* (I Corinthians 2:9)." So, according to scripture, God is not hiding his Kingdom from us, <u>but for those</u> who would love and obey him.

The human mind is not capable of seeing God's hidden treasure without the help of the Holy Spirit. We have to come to the Lord if we want what he has hidden for us. He does this in part, so that when the glory is revealed, no man can take credit for it. We cannot say that it was because of who were or what we have done. God has hidden his treasure so that without him, it cannot be found. And, why not? It's his treasure. If a ordinary man hid a treasure, you would have to either go to him or find his treasure map in order to learn its whereabouts. Same is true with God's most precious treasure. His treasure is more valuable than any earthly treasure. I am reminded of Jesus' parables, *"Again, the kingdom of heaven is like unto treasure hid in a field; the which when a man hath found, he hideth, and for joy thereof goeth and selleth all that he hath, and buyeth that field. Again, the kingdom of heaven is like unto a merchant man, seeking goodly pearls: Who, when he had found one pearl of great price, went and sold all that he had, and bought it.* (Matthew 13:44-46)." To obtain God's treasure, you have to go after it like great treasure. You have to be as one who is seeking precious jewels. There are relentlessly determined people who are ready to sell all they have to obtain God's treasure. Often Christians are waiting for God to drop his treasure on them. They hesitate to seek for it because they don't have faith enough to believe the word only. This sounds a lot like what Thomas said, when the other disciples told him about how they had seen the resurrected Jesus. *"But Thomas, one of the twelve, called Didymus, was not with them when Jesus came. The other disciples therefore said unto him, We have seen the Lord. But he said unto them, Except I shall see in his hands the print of the nails, and put my finger into the print of the nails, and thrust my hand into his side, I will not believe* (John 20:24-25)." Eight days later, Jesus appears to the disciples and tells Thomas to touch his wounds. It was then that he recognized the Lord. Then Jesus let him know that those who are truly blessed are those who have not seen and yet they have believed. *"Jesus saith unto him, Thomas, because thou hast seen me, thou hast believed: blessed are they that have not seen, and yet have believed* (John 20:26-29)."

The just shall live by faith. This is a command. Without faith, we cannot please God (Hebrews 11:6). When we exhibit our faith, God manifests himself to us. Still there are Christians who have more faith in technology than in God. Technology can give you information about God, but a close personal relationship brings you fresh revelation straight from the heart of God. He never said that upon technology I have built my church. When Peter received supernatural revelation about the true identity of Jesus Christ, he said, *"Thou art the Christ, the son of the living God." "And Jesus answered and said unto him, Blessed art thou, Simon Barjona: for flesh and blood hath not revealed it unto thee, but my Father which is in heaven. And I say also unto thee, That thou art Peter, and upon this rock I will build my church; and the gates of hell shall not prevail against it* (Matthew 16:13-18)." Jesus sent the Holy Spirit who brings to us revelation knowledge. Revelation is the rock that we need. It is the basis of our faith. It is the faith of God being revealed to our spirits. How great is that revelation? Jesus gave the parable of the mustard seed. *"The kingdom of heaven is like to a grain of mustard seed, which a man took, and sowed in his field: Which indeed is the least of all seeds: but when it is grown, it is the greatest among herbs, and becometh a tree, so that the birds of the air come and lodge in the branches thereof* (Matthew 13:31-32)." The word of the kingdom may seem quite small and insignificant to the ordinary person, but when it is received and comes to fruition, the harvest is vast. One word from God can transform your whole life in an instant. I recall the Lord telling me that his word was like a powerful mind sweeper. It can go to great depths of the human soul and detonate every deadly thing. Hebrews 4:12 says, *"For the word of God is quick, and powerful, and sharper than any twoedged sword, piercing even to the dividing asunder of soul and spirit, and of the joints and marrow, and is a discerner of the thoughts and intents of the heart."* No one can escape the power of God's word. In the book of Acts, whenever the word of the kingdom was preached, it caused multitudes to turn to the Lord (Acts 4:4, 5:14). My favorite is Acts 19:20 which reads, *"So mightily grew the word of God and prevailed."* Like a mustard seed, the word grew mightily and it prevailed. Now consider this. If a single mustard seed can produce a tree for birds to nest, just imagine what kind of habitation the word of God could create for one who has ears to hear and a heart to obey the word. Through his obedience, that person would make a habitation where God would dwell and manifest himself for an eternity. This is what it means to be in the secret place of the Most High and dwell under the shadow of the Almighty (Psalm 91:1).

One word from God can do that and more, even producing days of heaven upon the earth. This is the hidden power of the word. It may seem small and simple when it is spoken, but in the end it will produce great results. That is why it is necessary that we must speak and do whatever the Holy Spirit tells to speak and do. It is God's desire that the word be taken to the uttermost parts of the world, but how God chooses to disseminate the word, it up to him. There is great purpose behind God's mysteries. Those of us who are led by the Spirit of God, unveil those mysteries in our obedience. We may hear a simple word of instruction, and God reveals a mystery before our very eyes. Even then, we don't know all. The wisdom of God is infinite. We will never know just how far reaching our obedience has extended, but we do know that God uses mysteries for his divine purpose. For it is not the wisdom of men, but the wisdom of God that is packed with power. These are not known to mere men, but to those who are of the household of faith. The purpose of the mysteries is to demonstrate the power of God's Kingdom. The mysteries insure that no man can take credit for what God had planned before the foundation of the world. Even the life, death and resurrection of Jesus Christ was shrouded in a mystery. It wasn't until the Holy Spirit came to the earth that mysteries started being revealed to the apostles.

Perhaps the greatest hidden secret of God's Kingdom is the power of love. It's not that God has intentionally hidden his love, but that so few people actually accept his love and experience it for themselves. We talk about the love of God. For most, talking about love is all they will ever do. Many pastors and leaders of the church belittle the notion of love.

They can read John 3:16 and tell you that God so loved the world that he gave his only begotten son, but when it comes to loving God, and then loving your neighbor as Jesus commanded (Matthew 22:37-40), very few practice it. I observed real Kingdom love in the Baptist church. When it came loving and sharing with one another, I've never experienced any of God's people who did it better than the Baptist. Even so, there are many men in the church who think that love is weak. Preachers even make fun of love, and yet God **is** love.

God's love is such a powerful force that it can be most frightening at times. His love is not the human kind of love at all. For instance, it was the love of God that Adam and Eve were banished out of the garden and cursed. Why would I say that? God knew that if they had stayed in the garden and had eaten from the tree of life, all humanity would be doomed to the curse and death for an eternity. This was the grace of God; the proof that he loved humanity too much to let us stay in ruin. It was also God's love for us that caused him to send Jesus to die upon that cross, so that Adam's curse could be reversed for all humanity. How many fathers do you know love humanity enough to sacrifice their own son for some else's life? This is how much God loves us. Christians say they understand love, but until they truly have a one-on-one relationship with God, they won't have a clue as to what it means to love another person. Jesus said that the greatest love we can show one another is to lay down our lives for a friend (John 15:13). Most people love themselves so much that the notion of laying down their lives for others would never enter their minds. God's love is a sacrificial love. It is essential to getting anything from God's Kingdom.

Love is the key to unlocking everything in God has for us. Faith works by love (Galatians 5:6). If we love God and humanity, we will show it by our works. We will feed and clothe our neighbor in need, especially those in the household of faith. If we love, then we will take care of all those who are suffering and those who are less fortunate. In the Book of Acts this was demonstrated when people sold their houses and possessions and laid the proceeds at the feet of the apostles for distribution to those in need. There was great grace upon them, not because of what God did, but because they obeyed the Holy Spirit and walked in love with one another. The Bible says that in the early church, there was no one that lacked (Acts 4:33-35). Every need was met. We are commanded to love God first, and then to love one another as we love ourselves. Even

Jesus told his disciples that this was his one and only commandment; to love. He said that the world would know us by our love for one another (John 13:34-35). This is no ordinary human love. He commanded us to love another as he loved us. How did Jesus love us? He gave up his life for us. This is the greatest love we can show for one another. It doesn't necessarily mean that we have to die for another like Jesus died on the cross. It does mean that we must give of our lives, our wants and desires to help another. Sacrificial love is required of everyone who believes in Jesus Christ. Jesus made it very clear that if we want to have what he has, we must let go of every earthly thing to follow him. If we even love mother or father, sister, brother, children or anyone above him, we cannot be his disciples (Luke 14:26-27). To follow him, our love has to be focused on God, Jesus and the Kingdom plan. We are commanded to deny ourselves all earthly and fleshly desires. Then we are commanded to take up our cross and follow Jesus. This is real Kingdom love, when we can deny this world to follow in the footsteps of the one that gave his life for us. We love him because he first loved us and sacrificed his life for us (I John 4:19). That is where our loyalty lies, not in our earthly ties, but in the eternal bond of the spirit of life in Christ Jesus. We still love our neighbor and our families, but we love Jesus more. Our love for Jesus will bring a wellspring of prosperity, healing and deliverance to our families, and to the world around us.

Love is also a powerful weapon against the kingdom of darkness. Satan causes division and hatred in the church. The only thing that can defeat Satan's hold on us, is love. He does not understand love. It throws the devil for a loop every time. Love upsets his game, because love is not in him. Satan cannot not come against something that he does not understand. Love gives, while hatred takes away. Satan is a thief, who comes to steal, kill and destroy (John 10:10). Jesus on the other hand, came to give us abundant life, one that is filled with love for the father. If we love the father, then we will live as he lives and loves as he loves. God's love is tough to handle at times. It does not follow human reason or emotion. Obeying the Holy Spirit's command to pray is also an act of love. What American Christians don't seem understand is that if God is telling you to pray or to do something for someone, it is not about that person, it is about you. There may be a prayer that has never been answered and God would have you sow a seed in prayer during the wee hours of the morning. Don't get angry that God interrupted your sleep. Thank him that you have the opportunity to help someone else get their prayer answered. Don't question what God is showing you in the spirit. Pray in love and stay in love until the Holy Spirit releases you. God is requiring you to give sacrificially to another in their hour of need. When your time comes, you will have sufficient credit in your account to call upon in your time of need. When you obey with a grateful heart, there will always be a reward awaiting you. The call to faithful obedience is never hidden in the Kingdom, yet the reward is almost always hidden, on purpose. God wants to reward those who willing obey him. He tests us continually to see if we are ready to be elevated to the next level of glory.

In God's Kingdom we must abide in *faith*, and *hope* and in *love*. We can get nothing from God outside of *faith*. We must simply believe that he loves us, and that he will take care of us no matter what. His instructions to us are not for our harm, but they are for our good. We must have faith in his word. It is also necessary that we know the *hope* of his calling for our lives (Ephesians 1:18). This will certainly make the difference in your life. It will no longer be about you and your issues, but about God's call on your life. In fact, the Lord may even show how all your "issues" in life, were never about you, but about what he was calling you to do.

God will never cast you off. Instead, he has a wonderful plan for your life. This will become your motivation to continue on in the faith. God will give you hope. Remember, God is *love*. We must abide in faith, hope and in Him, but the greatest of these is *love* (I Corinthians 13:8,13). Only then, will the hidden Kingdom manifest in our lives, producing results far beyond anything we could ever ask or think.

BABYLON HAS FALLEN!

Religious Pride And Deception

For the purpose of spiritual comparison, the names Babylon and Satan can be used synonymously. It was Satan who started all this nonsense about rebelling against God. It wasn't enough to rebel on his own, but Satan led a rebellion. It not only pleased him to do that which was wrong, but he got pleasure in others who also did wrong (Romans 1:32). Satan's modus operandi is always to lead a rebellion against God. He has a flair for creating strife and division amongst men. He also enjoys turning men's hearts against God. He is like a master puppeteer who pulls people's strings, causing envy and confusion in God's family. The people don't know what they are doing. They are simply puppets on a demonic string. They are pawns of the kingdom of darkness. This is Satan's greatest pleasure. As long as he can influence brother to fight against brother and nation to rise up against nation, Satan gets pleasure in thinking that he has upset the plan of God. He is a prideful devil who believes that he is just as powerful as Almighty God. Every time he uses men as pawns, Satan glories in his power over God. It reminds him of how he led a rebellion in heaven. He is also a tenacious devil because he continues to act as if there are no consequences to his behavior. Somehow Satan has fooled himself in believing that God can do him no harm. Did he forget how God cast him out of heaven and exiled him to this earth? Jesus even talked about what happened, *"I beheld Satan as lightning fall from heaven (Luke 10:18)."* What will be God's final punishment for Satan? He will be cast into the lake of fire to be tormented day and night forever (Revelation 20:10). That was Satan, so what about Babylon?

Like Satan, Babylon is lifted up in pride. She says in her heart, *"I sit a queen, and am no widow, and shall see no sorrow* (Revelation 18:7).*"* This is how Babylon thinks. That spirit believes that since it has been successful in gaining wealth (even ill-gotten gain), and merchandising (of stolen wares), and fornicating, Babylon is on top of the world. In fact the Bible says that she is *"the great whore"* that sits upon many waters (Revelation 17:1). She is also said to sit upon seven mountains of this world (Revelation 17:9). Babylon's evil influence is worldwide. She has led a rebellion against God and is against everything that is holy. She sees her accomplishments worthy of her own throne. Does this sound familiar? It was Satan who said, *"I will ascend into heaven, I will exalt my throne above the stars of God: I will sit also upon the mount of the congregation, in the sides of the north: I will ascend above the heights of the clouds; I will be like the most High* (Isaiah 14:13-14).*"* This is exactly what Babylon is saying as well. This spirit not only exalts itself against God, but Babylon gets pleasure in persecuting and killing God's people. The Bible says that she is drunk on the blood of the saints and martyrs (Revelation 17:6).

Babylon, like Satan, hates God and everyone associated with God and his will for the earth. It's a spirit that is determined to prove that it is superior to God. Whatever God says do, Babylon says it can do better. This kind of pride finds its strength in numbers. Evil always seems to be undivided in its effort to come against that which is good. God's people appear to be passive, as Babylon aggressively forces people to turn against God in solidarity. How does this play out in the Babylonian Church in America? First of all, religious men always think that God is on their side. In their minds, what evil they do is for God. Take what happened in the ministry of Jesus. The Pharisees were always accusing Jesus of violating the law by working miracles on the Sabbath, yet while the miracle is in process these religious men were plotting Jesus' death. What happened to the supreme law that says, Do Not Kill? It's like Jesus said, those who kill you will think they are doing it in service to God. Why would anyone do such absurdity? They don't know God or Jesus Christ (John 16:2-3). Their pride has led them into deception. Pride has somehow closed their mind to see the obvious. Prideful, men are always blinded to the destruction that lays ahead. For the Bible says and demonstrates so clearly that pride comes before one falls (Proverbs 16:18). Remember that Babylon believes that it is invincible. Babylon thinks she will reign forever. That is a great deception. Man's time on earth is limited. No one reigns forever except for Jesus Christ and His Kingdom. Let no man think of himself more highly than he ought. God is the judge. He puts one person down and set up another (Psalm 75:7). God will put down one from his lofty seat and raise a lowly one to take his place (Luke 1:52). Pride lures men into hell, but God has a way of humbling even the most haughty person.

Take another look at religious men who in their pride have chosen to follow after traditions of men, instead of following after the example that Jesus Christ gave us to follow. These men are being lured into hell by Satan, that father of lies and master of deception. Jesus called them the blind leaders of the blind, in which they all will fall into the ditch (Matthew 15:14). Religious men always think that they are in agreement with God, simply by right of being in the church. It's as if they feel that God has given them Carte Blanche in the Kingdom, and whatever they desire will come to pass. Pride opens the door for self-righteousness to be magnified amongst religious men. They use it to intimidate the weak. Therefore, religious men will always find others who will agree with them, even in the most unholy schemes. Again, Babylon likes doing evil and enjoys it when others also do evil. Religious men enjoy forcing people to do evil. They will even exalt their authority to make you disobey God. I was in a church in which the pastor hated me. He hated my gifts and he hated the fact that I was a women. He took an opportunity to force me to do something that the Lord told the church not to do. The pastor set me up, hoping that God would punish me. What do you do when a superior tells you to do something that is forbidden? You go over his head, not to the bishop, nor to the elders, you take the matter to God in prayer. That is exactly what I did, and the Lord taught me a powerful message about divine authority. He told me that since I was in that church, I had to submit to the pastors wishes, even though what I was told to do was forbidden. The Lord told me to go ahead and do what the pastor asked, and he (God) would deal with the pastor about the trap he set for me. So, I did what the pastor asked. A few days later, the pastor stormed through the church in anger looking for me. Something happened and he just assumed that it happened because I disobeyed his orders. I gave him proof that I did exactly what he asked. He was confused for a moment because this man had hoped that something would happen to me, instead his plan backfired. I never knew what happened. I just knew that God kept his word and settled the matter himself.

The Babylonian system of operation, whether in the church or in this world, is a system of corruption. Babylon revels in its power to do things against God's will. Most of what is done is undercover, out of plain sight, but it is evil none the less. It's as if people think that God is blind, deaf and dumb. Their pride deceives them into believing that they got one over on God. Now here is why they feel that way. Babylon always assumes that everyone in the world thinks like she does; that everyone longs to do evil in their hearts, and at the first chance they will rebel against God. For the masses this is true, but God has a people who will not compromise. They will do what's right whether anyone is watching or not. They do right because it is the right thing to do. They want to please God. Babylon on the other hand, wants to do evil just because it can. It's the natural thing for her to do. Even in their arrogance, religious men will use the fear of God to coax people into doing evil. When religious men impose their evil desires upon others, this is the ultimate in terrorism. Their victims are overtaken in fear; the fear of God and the fear of retaliation of religious men. In my experience, religious men will even threaten you to your face, just like they did to Jesus. They have no shame in how they deal with those whom they hate. They act as though they are law enforcement and you are the criminal. I have had leaders rough me up and throw me into a room and lock the door. These were evil men doing the will of Satan to inflict harm upon me. In a recent magazine article I wrote about a female pastor who threw a punch at me from behind. It was after a service in which I was the guest speaker. My being there aroused the anger of another leader. While I was speaking to some people outside of the church, the Holy Spirit moved upon me in the most unusual way. In my natural senses, I never heard or felt any danger, but my right arm automatically moved across my body and over my left shoulder to block a punch that was thrown behind my head. I turned my head, after I felt the impact of someone's fist in my hand. There stood a demon possessed pastor who wanted to pick a fight on the church grounds. Her spirit was haughty as she offered to hurt me for taking her place in the pulpit. It was the devil causing this arrogant woman to act a fool in front of the congregation.

There was another time that I was attending a home Bible Study that was being led by leader who was also a prophetess at this church. She had a prophecy that came straight from heaven and everyone was blessed. When the woman sat down a spirit of pride came over her. I saw it because it caused a demon spirit to enter the room. Before the night was over that same woman was "prophe-lying" to everyone in the room. When she came my direction, I headed for the door. Then the Lord said, **"Protect your heart."** The woman said she had a word for me, but I told her that I was not interested. She took me by the wrist and pushed me into a chair and began speaking words straight from hell. I prayed about what happened that night and the Lord told me to continue interceding for the woman, and to inform the pastor about what happened. When I informed the pastor, he was outraged because evidently this kind of thing had happened in the past. During the next Bible Study, one of the elders was in attendance to make sure the devil was not going to be let loose again. Well, the prophetess was so angry that I told the pastor, that she began leaving threats on my family telephone recorder. She was threatening bodily harm because of what the Lord had me do. This went on for weeks. This woman was a prophetess who had a serious issue with pride. I experienced first hand, that pride is a devil willing to hurt another just to prove that is right. It is like being forced to comply with sin in a dysfunctional family. If people are forced to live with an evil for so long, many will begin to think that it must be the will of God. Weak minded Christians can be driven into condemnation and self punishment for even thinking that their leaders could do them harm. When in reality, the leaders are evil and God needs to intervene, but he will not intervene unless we go to him in prayer. Never rebuke an elder (I Timothy 5:1). Always take it to God in prayer.

We all know right from wrong based upon what we have learned in life. What we must realize is this. Just because someone holds a position in church, or because God uses them in the gifts of the spirit, does not mean that they are always right in their decisions. It also does not reflect their righteous position with God. The gifts of God are without repentance (Romans 11:29). Which means that once God has called someone and gifted them for his service, he won't take back what he has ordained. God will not change his mind about what he wants to do, but he may change how he gets that thing done. In an earlier discussion we talked about John the Baptist's comment to the Pharisees and Sadducees who were proud of their sonship with Abraham, thinking that it would exempt them from having to repent. John told them that God was able to raise up stones as children of Abraham (Luke 3:8). In that same discussion, we talked about what happened to Solomon. God gave his word to King David that his lineage would reign on the throne forever, but when Solomon sinned by marrying strange women, God had to do something. He could not repent for what he said to David, and yet he could not let sin reign over all of the people. God split the kingdom into two thrones.

King Solomon loved God. He vowed to walk in his ways, but at some point in his reign, pride took over and he refused to heed the word of the Lord. Unfortunately, the same happened with both Rehoboam and Jeroboam. They both did evil in the sight of God (I Kings Chapters 12-14). Being chosen by God brings with it great honor, and yet a heart full of pride will cause honor to turn into shame. Religious pride and deception have always been the downfall of God's people. Position and power, like riches, can be very deceiving. Leaders can be deceived into believing that they are autonomous. Very prominent leaders in the American Church often shut down revelation knowledge from God. Instead, they even prophesy what **they** want and not what the Lord wills. Those who prophesy from their human desires truly believe they are within their right to do so. They believe that they can declare a thing and it shall be established. But, what does the Word of God say? *"Receive, I pray thee, the law from his mouth, and lay up his words in thine heart. . . . For then thou shalt have thy delight in the Almighty, and shalt lift up thy face unto God. Thou shalt make thy prayer unto him, and he shall hear thee, and thou shalt pay thy vows. Thou shalt also decree a thing, and it shall be established unto thee: and the light shall shine upon thy ways* (Job 22:22-28)." Before one is able to declare a thing, he must line up his mouth with the Word of God. Prideful men, don't care for the fine detail in God's Word. These men decree and declare things that are perverse in the sight of God, and to a certain point, it seems as if they are getting away with it. How is it possible to be carried away with such deception? Men are lured by their lust for power, and because God does not immediately break up their plans, for a brief time, they are deceived into believing that they have more power than God. The Bible says that God laughs at the wicked who think they have gotten away with their schemes (Psalm 37:12-13). The Lord knows how it all will end. God will always have the last laugh.

There is another factor at play in this deception, and that is the power of agreement. Let's revisit what God said about the builders of the Tower of Babel. *"And the LORD said, Behold, the people is one, and they have all one language; and this they begin to do: and now nothing will be restrained from them, which they have imagined to do* (Genesis 11:6)." The power of agreement is a powerful force in this earth, but what happens if your agreement is in direct opposition with what God has commanded? It seems that God lets deception continue alongside the truth for a reason. You will find true teachers alongside false teachers; true prophets alongside false prophets in the church. There are wheat and tares growing in the same field. Jesus said it will remain that way until the time of the harvest (Matthew 13:30). There are prophetic seasons that God has appointed for judgement, when he rewards everyman according to his works. It's not the final judgment of the earth, but only a season of the harvest for the seeds one has sown. It is during these harvest seasons that God will show his powerful hand and scatter the proud in the imagination of their hearts (Luke 1:51). *"There is a way which seemeth right unto a man, but the end thereof are the ways of death (Proverbs 14:12; 16:25)."* We are in such a time. The Lord says that it is the **"Grande Finale"**[1] harvest before Jesus returns. Therefore God is calling upon his people to repent and turn their hearts back to him.

Since the sin of Adam, men have been inclined to think of themselves as gods. Consequently, they tend to reject the True and Living God. The Lord says that **"it's a matter of pride."** God would have us to beware of pride. We talk about "American Pride." We're "Proud to be American." Even parents often say that they are proud of their children, but what does God say about his son Jesus? *"This is my beloved Son, in whom I am well pleased* (Matthew 3:17)." Notice that God never said, he was proud of Jesus. Instead he said that in Jesus, he was well pleased. What is the highest compliment any believer could expect from God? He will never say that he is proud of us. God will simply say, *"Well done, good and faithful servant* (Matthew 25:23)." The Bible never talks about God being proud of his children. Instead it is often said that God has pleasure in his people (Psalm 35:27), or how he has joy or pleasure over us, but never is there any Biblical mention of God being proud of his children. The Lord brought this discussion of pride to my attention. He wanted me to stress the importance of his people avoiding pride. It is the epitome of self adulation. Even when God created the heavens and the earth and all that is in them, he never said that he was proud of his creation. Instead God observed all he created and said that is was *very good* (Genesis 1:31); that it brought pleasure to him. Revelation 4:11 says that God created everything for his purpose and his pleasure.

Pride is such an evil in the eyes of God. The Bible contains numerous warnings about the consequences of pride, and yet in all our human endeavors we value those who take pride in themselves, and who take pride in their work. How quick we are to look at the work of our hands without considering the Creator who gave us all that we possess. We've made our existence all about us, as if we created and endowed ourselves. This is idolatry for sure, when men worship and serve the creation more than the creator (Romans 1:25). I am reminded of the time the Children of Israel were preparing to enter the Promised Land. The Lord gave them a stern warning about remembering that it was he (God) that

---

1   Matthews, Paula. "Year 2002: The Enemy Exposed And God's Plan Revealed." *The War Journal (1999-2010) Volume I*. Los Angeles: Spirit & Life Publications, 2010. 181. Print.

provided everything for them. *"Beware that thou forget not the LORD thy God, in not keeping his commandments, and his judgments, and his statutes, which I command thee this day: Lest when thou hast eaten and art full, and hast built goodly houses, and dwelt therein; And when thy herds and thy flocks multiply, and thy silver and thy gold is multiplied, and all that thou hast is multiplied; Then thine heart be lifted up, and thou forget the LORD thy God, which brought thee forth out of the land of Egypt, from the house of bondage; . . . And thou say in thine heart, My power and the might of mine hand hath gotten me this wealth. But thou shalt remember the LORD thy God: for it is he that giveth thee power to get wealth, that he may establish his covenant which he sware unto thy fathers, as it is this day. And it shall be, if thou do at all forget the LORD thy God, and walk after other gods, and serve them, and worship them, I testify against you this day that ye shall surely perish. As the nations which the LORD destroyeth before your face, so shall ye perish; because ye would not be obedient unto the voice of the LORD your God* (Deuteronomy 8:11-20)." God made it plain to his people that in the day that they pridefully thought that they got everything by their own power, they would surely perish. God showed no mercy to his enemies in the wilderness. He not only killed them, but he also tore down their idols and burned them with fire. That gives you an idea of just how serious God is about those who disobey him. He said he would do the same to his own people if they forgot his commandments. Did they believe God? No!

Moses went up to the Mount Sinai to meet with God to get the ten commandments on stone. He was only gone forty days and forty nights. The people became restless. They asked Aaron, the priest, who was also Moses' brother, to make them an idol to worship since Moses was gone for so long. Aaron did what the people demanded. He made them an idol. The people said, *"These be thy gods, O Israel, which brought thee up out of the land of Egypt."* So what happened? Did they just choose not to remember what the Lord commanded? Did they not remember that in the day they would forget God, they would perish? Apparently they did. Even Aaron seemed to be going along with the people's wishes. After he made the golden calf, he declared that the next day they would make a feast unto the Lord (Exodus 32:1-35). Eventually, all the men of Israel over the age of twenty-one were killed in the wilderness. It was their children that went in and possessed the land that God swore to give their fathers (Joshua 5:6-7). God showed mercy during that time and will do so in our day. Because the rebellion in America has lasted so long, it has impeded the Kingdom progress. There are those who are crying out to God to go into their own promised lands, and the only thing in the way is the rebellious men in the church. They want to stay encamped in the wilderness, but God has another plan. It's a plan that will go forth, with or without them. The church has also chosen to deliberately sin against God. They are not so concerned about God's Kingdom agenda. They are more interested in their own fleshly desires. The church is steeped in idolatry. Like those who were slain in the wilderness, they also permit fornication. They murmur and complain against God and his leaders. It's only by the grace of God that the entire lot has not been slain. God has given them grace, but this is the last season. The judgment of God has been issued against the church. The church is also quite prideful. Pride is a satanic plot against human kind; against one's own destiny. Satan knows exactly what happens to those who exalt their thrones above God. Pride is what got him kicked out of heaven (Revelation 12:9). In fact, it gives him great pleasure to lead men to rebel against God because he knows that men will fall as he did. That is what happened to Adam. Pride of life and the lust of the flesh (I John 2:16) cost him his destiny.

The American Church could learn a valuable lesson from Adam's failure. Although the Church has been placed in the world to "tend and keep it," many Christians have been taught that we can depart from that commandment, to do our own thing. Like Adam, the church has left its divine responsibility to tend to its own lust of the flesh, the lust of the eyes and the pride of American life. At first glance, the hypocrisy and rebellion of the American Church was quite perplexing to me because the Bible is very clear about our responsibility under God. Then again, most American Churches don't follow the Bible in its entirety. They pick and choose what they want to believe and discard the rest. In general, the American Church follows after the traditions of men which renders the word of God null and void (Mark 7:9). The church is very deceptive through rituals and religion. We look good on the outside, but our hearts are desperately wicked, but who would know it? God knows, because he searches the hearts of men (Jeremiah 17:9-10). It is that which comes from inside the heart of man that defiles him. *"For from within, out of the heart of men, proceed evil thoughts, adulteries, fornications, murders, Thefts, covetousness, wickedness, deceit, lasciviousness, an evil eye, blasphemy, pride, foolishness: All these evil things come from within, and defile the man* (Mark 7:21-23)." When that heart is not singularly focused on the purpose and plan of God, the body walks in darkness. *"The light of the body is the eye: if therefore thine eye be single, thy whole body shall be full of light. But if thine eye be evil, thy whole body shall be full of darkness. If therefore the light that is in thee be darkness, how great [is] that darkness* (Matthew 6:22-23)*!"* So, while there is a way that seems right to a man, the end of that road is death. God is beckoning his people to depart from their prideful ways, and humble themselves before him, not only for the sake of the church, but for the sake of the Kingdom, America and the nations of the earth.

"If my people, which are called by my name, shall humble themselves, and pray, and seek my face, and turn from their wicked ways; then will I hear from heaven, and will forgive their sin, and will heal their land." I I Chronicles 7:14

The American Dream Turned Nightmare

The spirit of Babylon emanates from the church and permeates throughout our nation. American Christians are seemingly more susceptible to this spirit than Christians from other cultures. In United States, we have created our own *Tower of Babel* called the American Dream. Many believe that in America, everyone has an equal opportunity to achieve success and prosperity with hard work and determination. We applaud the effort of human beings, without recognizing the Creator who endowed us. It is a thing of pride to be called a "self-made" individual. What does it mean to be a self-made millionaire or a self-made billionaire in America? The implication is that they alone were responsible for their own success; that no one, including Almighty God assisted them in gaining their level of status. This is absurdity. Did we create ourselves? Did we design our own mental and physical capacities? Where did those successful ideas comes from? Even the most creative ideas comes from the Creator. No individual is acting alone in this world. There are unseen forces of influences that guide us to our particular end. The spirit of Babylon is such an influence. It is a demonic spirit that operates in trafficking and illegal merchandising of stolen goods. Babylon believes that the end justifies the means, therefore everything goes. She entices competition for items she does not own, hoping to get the best deal from the highest bidder by fraud. Babylon is like a slave owner keeping her harlots at competition with earth other, lusting after that which she does not own. It's all about the bottom line; making a profit at all costs. Unfortunately Americans rarely talk about the cost of that success. No one wants to talk about how it is acceptable in our nation to trample upon others on your way to success, and yet that is how our nation has gained most of its power. We have laid down a pattern of corruption in America that is not pleasing to God.

There is a particular Bible story that comes to mind. It is a story about King Ahab and his manipulative wife Jezebel (I Kings 21:1-16). Ahab was considered more evil than any king that ruled over God's people. Jezebel was a witch, even though she considered herself to be a prophetess of the idol Baal (Revelation 2:20). Ahab and Jezebel had a way of stirring up evil in one another. There was a man named Naboth who had a vineyard next to the palace. Ahab offered to buy the vineyard, but

Naboth refused. The king was so upset that he went home and pouted by refusing to eat. This stirred up Jezebel to take action. She drafted letters in Ahab's name announcing the public trial of Naboth for blaspheming God and the king. Jezebel set two false witnesses against Naboth. He was found guilty and stoned to death. When she learned that Naboth was dead, Jezebel sent Ahab to claim the vineyard. This story came to mind because it is reminiscent of how America was formed. In many instances, we still do business this way.

From its inception, America was a land cultivated by rebels and rogues. Many of the rebels were fleeing religious persecution in England. They desired to find a new land in which they could exercise their faith in the manner **they** chose. The early settlers also included opportunists who were looking for people and goods they could exploit for a profit. Although some would argue that America was a Christian nation, history shows that quite the opposite was true. Indeed, there was a strong religious influence from Christianity. We can see it in our laws and it has been engraved on our monuments, but American history records that what was engraved upon the hearts of its people was something of a mixture. America adopted religion instead of the true spirit of Christianity as Jesus taught. Religion corrupts and kills a people. We saw that in the Salem witch hunts when people were burned at the stake. We saw it when churches began segregating people based upon denomination and religious belief. We used the Bible to make treaties with the Native Americans. Then we disregarded those treaties and forced the people off of their lands, corralling them onto reservations like herds of animals. Those who resisted were killed in cold blood. The Bible teaches that all men were created in the image and likeness of God (Genesis 1:27), yet it was Christian men who used that same Bible to enslave and exploit generations of Africans who were forced to leave their country and endure inhumane treatment in America. We killed our brothers in the Civil War, where both sides used the Bible to justify their actions for and against slavery. This same America started missions in the Hawaiian Islands. We taught them about Jesus, then used our military strength to overthrow their government and forcibly take their land for our possession. The Hawaiians who defended themselves were massacred. This is how the American Dream was fulfilled in the lives of those who took power and possession of this New Land.

America has a long history of exploiting nations and people whom we deemed less important than ourselves. The term that comes to mind is *supremacy*. Many would call it *white supremacy*, but it is has deeper roots than that. It goes back to the religious spirit. We have seen it exercised by the white race over nonwhites, but it has its root in religion. This is religious extremism at its worst. Hitler used it against the Jews. America used it against people of color. It was so prevalent that it spawned decades of unrestrained activity by groups like the Klu Klux Klan, who were so bold as to wear white sheets over their heads as they carried burning crosses. Their so called religious attempts at ridding America of the "cursed" Blacks who were dirtying the land, was outrageously tolerated in our nation. No one seemed to care that the American Dream was not being realized for victims of these heinous crimes, yet a segment of our population was being slowly exterminated by lynching. Fast forward to year 2001, when the twin towers were destroyed by yet another religious group's attempt to purify the world of America's evil. Our lust for the American Dream has enraged our enemies. People will hate you because you have more wealth than they do, but when you brag about the immoral or corrupt way you obtained that wealth, it inflames them even more.

Here is the twist on America. We believe that God has blessed us to be exceptional in this world. We want him to bless us, but in our nation, there are so many ways to be prosperous without God. Even Christians get confused. They will walk according to the world's standards, and call it the Blessing of God. That is akin to Lot seeing Sodom and Gomorrah, and calling it the garden of the Lord (Genesis 13:10). How do we know the difference? The Bible says that the Blessing of the Lord brings wealth without sorrow (Proverbs 10:22). The sorrow mentioned here is the backlash of the curse for having taken from others. It is the result of one doing as Jezebel and Ahab did in taking from Naboth. When an evil is done against another, especially when it is done to an innocent party, God takes note. Even the blood of the innocent cries out to God beyond the grave calling for justice (Genesis 4:10). That is what happened in the story of Naboth. God sent Elijah the prophet to the vineyard where Ahab was taking possession, saying, *"Thus saith the LORD, In the place where dogs licked the blood of Naboth shall dogs lick thy blood, even thine* (I Kings 21:19). " Eventually, both Ahab and Jezebel were killed because of this, and other abominable acts against God. This is an example of how one gains wealth with sorrow. This is a curse and not the Blessing. We see this all around our nation. There is great financial wealth in some areas and great poverty and suffering in others. If the Blessing were working in our nation, there would be no sorrow, lack or suffering around us because those with the wealth would have more than money as a motivation. They would have the common good of all mankind at the center of their financial transactions. Most Americans (including Christians) are selfish. They don't even go to God for assistance. They see the Federal Government as their god. This is the *Tower of Babel* we have created, yet disillusionment abounds. *"When people talk about the "American Dream" it as if it's only an illusion. Unfortunately our nation has never found a solid ideology that could propel us back to greatness. Americans have become very self serving and indulgent. We've become a nation of takers, not givers. Everyone feels a sense of entitlement, like the government owes him or her. The wealthy won't give up their tax breaks, ministries won't give up their tax-exempt status and the poor won't give up their welfare, and no one is willing to give up their social security."*[1] Babylon is falling in the government because the people are no longer one. There are many voices speaking against the illegal and unethical practices of business and government. The wealth America has gained brought along with it, much sorrow; poverty, drugs, sex trafficking, rapidly inflated prices on consumer goods, stagnant salaries, and joblessness. This should be enough proof that the American Dream and the Blessing of God are not the same thing. Gone is the time that Americans revere God while they achieve what they did. People still say "God Bless America," but they have no idea if God will bless them or not. There is ideological confusion amongst American Christians who strive to do their own thing in life, and beg God to bless them. Even the words, "God Bless You" have no more meaning that it does when we say "God Bless America." Without obedience to God's word; there is no Blessing.

The American Dream, like the Blessing of God has ceased for all those who took God out of the picture. They have ceased because men have more faith in themselves and their own abilities, than faith in the God who is the giver of every good gift and ability in this earth. The Blessing of God requires that we trust in God's strength to achieve possessions and position. That means we must go back to our motto: "In God We Trust." We must trust God as our source for everything necessary

---

[1]   Matthews, Paula. "God's Kingdom Economics." *American Heritage 101*, Shaker Heights: Spirit & Life Publications[SM], 2012. 47. Print

for life. God must be our <u>only</u> source, if we want that same Blessing to correct the corruption left upon our nation because of the curse. People also have to be re-educated about why God gives us wealth. Christians often pray and hope that God would give them the house with the car, the family and the successful job to elevate themselves in the eyes of the world. God **will** give us those things, but with his Kingdom purpose in mind. He requires the same thing he required of the Children of Israel before they entered into the Promised Land. God wants us to remember that it was **he** that gave us the power to get wealth for the purposes of fulfilling his covenant with us (Deuteronomy 8:18). God wants the glory for what we do.

Babylon believes that fulfilling personal desires is of utmost importance. That is why the world is obsessed with lust. Lust is a demon from hell. Whether it is lust of the flesh, lust of the eyes, or the pride of life (I John 2:16), they all are characteristics of Babylon. Many people even feel powerless against the pressure of lust, so they automatically conform. Lust comes upon people with an insatiable pressure to be covetous; coveting what someone else has, coveting what we think will make us important in this world. People and things don't make us important. It is our relationship with God that makes us important. When we know God, he will Bless us, and make our names great. He also promises to make us a Blessing to the world (Genesis 12:1-2). God's dream for America is to bless us, but we must put him first, before ourselves. Then, God will make us such a blessing, that we will be able to bless all the nations of the world. That is God's plan for wealth. It's not about us. It's bigger than us. It includes the entire world.

God gave Joseph such a dream. On the surface, it looked like a dream that would raise Joseph up to rule over his family, but in reality he was elevated because God gave him a way to save the entire world from famine. Again, we go back to the Kingdom being like a mustard seed. It appears small and insignificant, but in the end it produces something larger than human imagination that solves an issue in the world. This is what happens when men achieve what God desires rather than pursuing their own personal gain. Babylon is about self. God's Blessing is about the world. What happened with Joseph was not unusual. This is how God operates in the lives of those who obey him.

It all starts with a dream, a vision or a word about what heaven desires for one's life on earth; and it almost always looks like an impossible dream. How would Joseph become ruler in Egypt when he was sold as a slave and imprisoned for all of those years? How was Esther, a Jewish commoner going to be queen in a foreign land? How would Abram from Ur of the Chaldees leave his family and follow the voice of God to a foreign land? How would he at his old age believe himself to be the father of many nations, when he didn't even have a child, and his wife was old and barren? How could a humble girl give birth to a child when she had never been with a man? How then could this child be called the Son of God? This is how the Kingdom of God operates. God uses simple people and things and makes them great. God uses a foolish things of this world to confound those who think they are wise (I Corinthians 1:27). He takes someone and something so insignificant, and uses them for his glory. It seems like the person or thing appeared out of no where. Truth is, a seed of faith was sown and was taking root long before the great harvest appeared. God had been maneuvering people and things into the right order; so that the harvest could manifest what he desires in the earth at the appointed time and season.

What God manifests is always greater than anything we could ask or think. That is why it is most beneficial to the world, that we follow God and not men. Men are limited by their intelligence and human capabilities. God is infinite in wisdom and capable of doing the impossible. God gives his children in impossible dream. In fact, most of the major inventions of our time were given to God's people first, but they failed to act upon them. Why? Religion held them back. Not understanding how the Kingdom operates also hindered them. The biggest excuse given for not doing what God desired, is the pursuit of the American Dream. God's people are pursuing jobs and career success. At a glance, it would seem admirable, but from the Kingdom point of view it is negligence. Why negligence? God ordered this world so that nothing would be lacking. If we had followed his order, poverty would not exist. Crime would be significantly diminished. People would be healed and in their right minds. The American Dream, applies pressure upon people to become successful and to get wealth by covetousness. That is why drugs and people are being trafficked. That is why criminals are stealing. Babylon says it is an all or nothing world. It pits people against one another to get their piece of the pie. God never created this world to lack in any way. Everything was designed from the very beginning to sustain itself for an eternity. The Blessing called for everything in this earth to be *fruitful and multiply, replenishing* itself. If things are being depleted, it is because of the curse. Babylon proliferates the curse. She tells one that the only way to get ahead is to take from others; steal their goods and sell them at a profit, steal their husbands because there aren't enough men in the world. Steal their money because they have too much and you don't have enough. The American Dream may have been a good idea from the start, but here is where we are now. Americans have trampled over too many people to obtain their success. This dream has become a nightmare. In the meanwhile, God's people are captivated with what they see in this world. Instead of speaking God's word and doing what he says, they speak what the world speaks and do what the world does. So, the earth is still in need of replenishing, but those who have the Blessing are not operating in it. Therefore poverty continues to increase. Suffering increases while everyone continues on the treadmill of lack in America. Truth is, THERE IS NO LACK IN AMERICA! The Spirit of God says that *there is no lack of resources* in this world, only a lack of obedient people willing to share their resources with others. Americans are hoarding the wealth while their neighbors are starving. They do this because they have also bought into the Babylonian idea that resources are limited. The greatest hindrance to the Gospel of Jesus Christ in America, IS AMERICA! We have created a *Tower of Babel* that must fall if this nation is to survive. God says that it must begin with the American Church. Their Tower of Religion has to fall. Then the Blessing must be utilized by those who are walking in faith; the same faith that caused Almighty God to see darkness and call Light into the world. God's people must get out of religion and speak what God is speaking and then we will see it manifested in this earth.

Here is the issue, God never wanted his children to toil and sorrow over money. It was never his intent that we try to make ends meet or that we make a living. God created a garden filled with pleasures for man. This was the original plan for human kind. Struggling and toiling was never in God's plan. It still isn't his plan for our lives. That is why God gives us dreams and visions about another way to live that is filled with the Blessing. Living life God's way, we will always prosper because the Blessing empowers us to prosper at all things. The problem is that America Christians talk about being blessed like the rest of the country does. Few have ever actually lived in the Blessing because it requires that we *"hearken to the voice of God."* Here is what the Bible says,

"And it shall come to pass, if thou shalt hearken diligently unto the voice of the LORD thy God, to observe and to do all his commandments which I command thee this day, that the LORD thy God will set thee on high above all nations of the earth: And all these blessings shall come on thee, and overtake thee, if thou shalt hearken unto the voice of the LORD thy God (Deuteronomy 28:1-2)." Here is another scripture that echoes the same message, *"If ye be willing and obedient, ye shall eat the good of the land* (Isaiah 1:19)." Jesus also said, *"If ye abide in me, and my words abide in you, ye shall ask what ye will, and it shall be done unto you* (John 15:7)." *". . . blessed are they that hear the word of God, and keep it* (Luke 11:28)." The Blessing comes only by hearing and obeying God.

The Blessing provides *eternal life*. Unfortunately, most believe it is available only in heaven. *Eternal life* is the supernatural life of God that flows from heaven upon the lives of every believer. It is the power of the Holy Spirit to transform life on earth, when one acts in faith on God's word. *Eternal Life* was intended to be a way of escaping the corruption and lack in this world. It restores all things to the peace and prosperity of Eden. It provides for us, the same life that Adam experienced before he sinned. God simply restored to mankind the life that was always intended for us here on earth. Remember that Jesus came to return Eternal life to us. What was included in that life? Jesus died to receive, *"to receive power, and riches, and wisdom, and strength, and honour, and glory, and blessing."* That is what Revelation 5:12 says. Jesus received all these things on our behalf. What does this have to do with being saved? You are being saved from the corruption of this world. It's more than just saying a prayer. God intends for his people to be a beacon of light for the world. He wants them to see our good works and glorify him (Matthew 5:16). We don't glorify God when we walk powerless in this world, living in poverty or barely making it, struggling like the rest of the world. If you are walking dishonorably like a fool and in the same curse, why would they ask you for help? Why would they come to your light? It would be too dim to see, if you hid it under a bush, or rarely lit it at all. This is where most Christians live. We have a ticket to heaven, but we live like hell on earth. That makes for a poor witness for Jesus Christ. We sit by and watch as the world is getting wealth through corruption and we do nothing. God gave us a plan, but no one seems to know how to work the plan. We pray, but we don't obey. Therefore you cannot obtain the good of the land. So, what is the solution? Christians need to get saved. I mean really saved according to how God designed his Kingdom. Americans need to give their lives to Jesus Christ and live out the life he died to give them. **This** is our inheritance. Religion has taught that God does not care about the things in this world, so God's people are happy living in lack, in pain and sickness, while cohabiting with the demons instead of making a habitation for the Lord Jesus. Christians are totally content in their ignorance, as they claim to be "suffering" for Jesus. In reality, they are suffering due to ignorance to what Jesus died to restore to them. He has placed wealth and abundance in the accounts of every believer, but few are making withdrawals. It's just sitting there. The cures for diseases and for poverty are just sitting there. The inventions, the specialized schools and businesses have never seen the light of day. These things are just sitting in an account with someone's name on it. They even refuse to inquire about what God has for them. The world is waiting for these things. Just by listening and obeying God, one of these ideas would make some child of God very wealthy. That was how God designed it. The world saw things and ran after them, but they were not qualified to do it God's way. They created the businesses and started the inventions and schools, but they did it under the curse. They still got the wealth because in the short term, these things met a need in society. Since it was done by the flesh and not by the spirit, it will eventually reap corruption (Galatians 6:8). It was done by Babylon's rules and therefore it must fall. No matter how important these things have been to society, Babylon must fall.

We see this throughout America. We have amassed great wealth, but our people are increasing in moral corruption. The rich are getting richer and the poor are suffering in greater numbers, and no one seems to care. This **is not** how God created this earth. God gave each of us gifts and talents that were designed to solve every issue in this earth. The Blessing would have replenished what needed to be done. It would have multiplied that which appeared to be scarce. Now, the nations of the earth are suffering, because Christians did not obey. Babylon is selfish and does not care. The people are suffering even more as they watch evil people get more wealth. This has caused crime to rise. Hatred and anger can be seen everywhere. Racial tensions are high because the economic issues coincide with race relations, especially when it appears that one race has all the wealth and power. These conditions also cause underground economies to flourish in illegal activities. More people are selling drugs and illegal contraband just for the money. Babylon has set this thing in a tail spin, but God gave the answers to the church. The answer starts with education. The church needs to be reeducated about the gospel. They need to go back read how Jesus said we would do greater works than he did (John 14:12). What did Jesus do? He healed the sick and cast out demons, caused the lame to walk, the maimed were healed and the dead were raised. These are the first things people think of when they hear the name of Jesus, but he did so much more. Remember that he increased Peter's fishing business and also paid his taxes for him. Jesus multiplied food to feed the multitudes. He calmed the stormy seas. According to Jesus, all his believers are supposed to be doing these, and even greater works than these. *"And these signs shall follow them that believe; In my name shall they cast out devils; they shall speak with new tongues; They shall take up serpents; and if they drink any deadly thing, it shall not hurt them; they shall lay hands on the sick, and they shall recover* (Mark 16:17-18).*"* This is what God expects from those who say they believe in Jesus Christ. What is the reality? Most of those who say they are believers, **don't** actually believe. Oh, they believe that Jesus can do these things. They also believe that great men and women of God can do these things, but most Christians do not believe they can do those things. In fact, it's even deeper than that. Jesus told his disciples, *"Heal the sick, cleanse the lepers, raise the dead, cast out devils: freely ye have received, freely give* (Matthew 10:8).*"* Simply put, you cannot give what you have not received. How can believers heal others when they have never received healing for themselves? They can't! Again, they believe God can do it, but they are not sure he will do it for them.

The American Church has taught its congregations to doubt God and what he did through Jesus Christ. They believe he can save them from sins and keep them out of hell. That part they believe, but getting them to believe anything else would require a miracle from heaven. Even then, some would not believe, because they have been taught not to believe in miracles too. So, if you don't believe in miracles, why would anyone need God? If you don't believe that Jesus and the Holy Spirit <u>can do through you</u> what he said **he would do**, how would you ever be able to let your light shine through your good works? Sure, you can feed the poor and clothe the naked, but people need more than physical comfort and provision. They need hope that God has not forsaken them. They need hope and assurance that God's word is true . . . but if believers don't actually believe, how can they help others to believe? Where is the witness? Where are the miracles, signs and wonders Jesus said would follow them? We saw them in the book of Acts, but not many in America. We see some signs that God has not forsaken us, but the vast majority of signs and wonders are being demonstrated in other countries of the Middle East and in Africa? Why there, and not in America? Those countries are desperately seeking help from God. Muslims are coming to Jesus in record numbers. The oppression in their countries has forced many to fall on their knees crying out to God. Allah is not answering their prayers, Jesus Christ is. He is showing up and appearing to them. When was the last time we heard of such miracles in America? This type of witness is virtually unheard of in America because we are so wrapped up in obtaining our American Dream, that we don't have time to seek after God.

In Babylonian America, the government and the employer have become the working man's god. Even American Christians have more faith in their jobs and in the federal government than they do in Almighty God. They believe the government can help them, but they don't believe that God will solve their issues. Many pastors refuse to take care of their own poor. They send them to the government instead. What would Jesus do? When the multitudes followed Jesus, and had not eaten in such a long period of time, **the disciples wanted to send the people away**, but Jesus had another plan. *"They need not depart; give ye them to eat (Matthew 14:16)."* Jesus had the disciples multiply the fish and the loaves to feed the people. In America, pastors don't necessarily need to multiply fish and loaves, but they could share what they have with their congregations. They could also teach their congregations to share with one another. Instead of doing what Jesus says do, these pastors will send their poor to the welfare offices and let the government handle it. Now, the people worship the government as provider instead of God. Why should we be surprised that Christians know that God can do something, but they are not sure he will do it for them? It's being reinforced by their pastors and leaders. God is not going to step out of heaven to feed the people. Jesus already did that. He came to earth to show us how to live in God's Kingdom. Jesus performed miracles as he listened to the voice of God and obeyed the commands of the Holy Spirit. That is what the American Church is called to do, but they refuse to do it. Some Christians will take the promises of God and use their own efforts in an attempt to bring it to pass. Babylon says that you can achieve anything if you work hard at it, right? Wrong! That is the way of the world, not of the Kingdom. Jesus said that it is the Father who does the work (John 14:10), not us. All we have to do is listen to the Lord and obey. As believers, we are called to speak what he says speak and do what he says to do. This is how the supernatural works. Babylon says that in America you have freedom of speech, that you can say and do whatever you want. You may have that legal right in America, but in the Kingdom, that same right would bring the curse upon your life. In America, people are doing their own will. In the Kingdom we are called to do the will of the Father. It's God's Kingdom agenda that is exalted, not our own. Jesus didn't even do his own will on earth. *"Verily, verily, I say unto you, The Son can do nothing of himself, but what he seeth the Father do: for what things soever he doeth, these also doeth the Son likewise* (John 5:19)." If we push our own agenda, it is the same as exalting our own throne. Satan exalted his throne and was kicked out of heaven (Revelation 12:9). Babylon exalted its throne and God confused their language and scattered them throughout the world (Genesis 11:8). We cannot change the world if we consider it our financial source. We cannot change ourselves unless we yield to the Holy Spirit and obey the word. In God's Kingdom, we can do nothing on our own. The promises of God simply cannot be obtained without doing things God's way.

There is nothing intrinsically wrong with the *work* ethic. It brings some success, but in the long term it becomes ineffective. That is why so many Americans are disillusioned with the American Dream. God's Kingdom believes that men should cease from their own labor and should work towards the rest that God's Blessing provides (Hebrews 4:10). We must strive to let God do the work in us. Babylon has men working for the money. This is slave labor. The Blessing has men working towards a destiny, giving them freedom in God's Kingdom. Now, God is not against hard work; as long as it is work he ordained for our lives. Christians believe that if you work hard, you can achieve anything in America. We cannot do anything we want just because of hard work, not if we want the destiny that God purposed for our lives. You can continue with the Babylonian system, but it is failing even as we speak. It was never meant to last forever. Nothing in this world lasts forever except for **that** which God ordains. Babylon is falling not only in America, but all across the world. There are nations in perpetual financial default. Other nations keep bailing them out. America has been borrowing more and more money from other countries as well. At some point, the lenders will call in all the loans. What happens then? The Babylonian system in America has had some success, but where it failed, most politicians tended to contain the situation just enough to keep things working until the next administration comes into office. America always passes its issues off to the next political administration, and no one ever seems to solve our financial issues. There is no solution in Babylon. The solution is in the Kingdom. Babylon does not know what to do. That is why America and the economies of the world are failing. God is about to bring mere men to their knees and let them know that **without him we can do nothing** (John 15:5). He knew this would happen. God will prove that his way to be superior. He will give solutions to his people to take up where the government and businesses have failed.

God created this world with a specific order. He gifted each of us so that we could bless the world. Now imagine what would happen, if those gifted at law decided that they wanted to cut lawn instead? What if those gifted as gardeners decided they wanted to operate the banks instead? Who would do the gardening? Who would represent us in legal matters? This sounds like a ridiculous example, but consider what is happening in America. If you talk to the average teenager, no one is talking about going to college. Most will tell you they want to be a dancer or a performer like those they see on television. What if they are gifted for technology and refuse to follow their gifts? Who will be attending our technology schools? Foreigners. That is exactly what has been happening. If America continues to be a lazy consumer of life, and refuses to contribute to the productivity of our nation, we will loose our edge. We already see that happening. What does it mean to buy American, when our goods and services are being produced in other nations where the labor is cheap? Other countries are delighted to do the work that Americans refuse to do, but our nation is being financially eroded from the inside out. They are so busy trying to make ends meet, that the average American just assumes that our nation will always be healthy. Not true. The nation is not healthy and has not been healthy for decades. People complain about the national debt. Well, consider the debt of the average American. We have been trained to be borrowers and not lenders. The Bible says **it is a curse** to be the borrower (Deuteronomy 28:43-44). Babylon says that borrowing someone else's money is the best way to make a profit. God says that under the Blessing, he would open his treasury and give us so much abundance that we would lend to many nations, and shall not borrow (Deuteronomy 28:12). God's treasure is unlimited. The United States Treasury is very limited and even overdrawn as we speak. ***"It shall fail,"*** says God, ***"and when it does, where***

will you turn?" Babylonian systems will fail all over the world, but here it the good news. **God has a plan for such a time as this**. In the past, men have promoted men; but in these last days, God will set some up and put others down. We are also about to see the greatest transfer of wealth that this world has ever seen. All the wealth that has been accumulated by evil men, will be supernaturally transferred into the hands of those who will honor God by taking care of the poor (Proverbs 28:8). The wealth of the sinner has always been accumulated but eventually it was destined to be given to the just (Proverbs 13:22). The Apostle James said, *"Go to now, [ye] rich men, weep and howl for your miseries that shall come upon [you]. Your riches are corrupted, and your garments are motheaten. Your gold and silver is cankered; and the rust of them shall be a witness against you, and shall eat your flesh as it were fire. Ye have heaped treasure together for the last days. Behold, the hire of the labourers who have reaped down your fields, which is of you kept back by fraud, crieth: and the cries of them which have reaped are entered into the ears of the Lord of sabaoth. Ye have lived in pleasure on the earth, and been wanton; ye have nourished your hearts, as in a day of slaughter. Ye have condemned [and] killed the just; [and] he doth not resist you. Be patient therefore, brethren, unto the coming of the Lord. Behold, the husbandman waiteth for the precious fruit of the earth, and hath long patience for it, until he receive the early and latter rain* (James 5:1-7).*"* God's Kingdom is the only refuge from the evil days to come. If you are one who is hurting the poor, repent. If you are cheating your employees, or cheating anyone from what is due them, you also need to repent. Purify your hearts, or else God will take all you have and give it to someone who pleases him.

What is coming in these last days is a move of God's Spirit upon the earth and its people. This will be a supernatural battle for the hearts of men. It is the desire of God that all men would be saved and come into the knowledge of the truth (I Timothy 2:4). What truth? The Lord wants the world to know the truth about why Jesus came. To let them know there is another way to live in this world, a way that is abundant and pleasing to God. Pleasing God is not in Babylon's agenda, but it will become more important in these last days. As we said earlier, the Blessing of God brings one into a place of wealth, without the sorrow and toil. Babylon provides a way to get wealth that looks deceptively easy, but in time, the pain and sorrow comes forth. What Babylon offers is not lasting. On the other hand, what God offers is *eternal*; there is no end. Babylon knows that her time is short, so she goes for the maximum impact in the shortest period of time. That is what lures men into her trap. She offers maximum pleasure and advertises a minimum price. This kind of seduction always captures simple men who are looking at today and not the consequences of tomorrow. Babylon knows what is coming, but it is of no concern for her agenda, because if one man falls, there will always be another to take his place. There is always someone who will fall in her trap. Babylon's desire is to keep men distracted with the deceitfulness of riches, which ultimately leads to their destruction.

The Lord wants his people out of Babylon so they can begin living and demonstrating the truth before all men. God is saying to the American Church, *"Come out of her my people* (Revelation 18:4)." Babylon will be destroyed and so will all those who remain with her at the time of her judgment. God's people have to get out, or they will be destroyed along with her. How can God's people escape? How can they get off this road to destruction? They have to change their hearts and let God in. *"Behold, I stand at the door, and knock: if any man hear my voice, and open the door, I will come in to him, and will sup with him, and he with me* (Revelation 3:20)." Remember that the Babylonian church is steep in religion. They do what they do, because they don't know God. They are missing the main reason Jesus came to earth. It's not about religion. Jesus came to restore a relationship between God and man. This is the truth that even the church had never known. This is about restoring God to his family, the family that Adam was suppose to spawn in this earth. Babylon is called the *Mother of Harlots* (Revelation 17:5). She has spawn a seed after her own kind. They are a rebellious lot who want to prove that they are equal to, if not better than God. The trap is that they are arrogant in their own wisdom and their own efforts. It even seems natural and right to them, but as the Bible says, *"There is a way that seems right to a man, But its end is the way of death* (Proverbs 14:12)." Man's way always leads to death. God offers a sure thing that can only lead to abundant life. He has even given us a way to escape the path of destruction, but it requires that we turn over the reigns of our lives to him and cease doing our own thing. God's way also requires that we have absolute trust in him. We must believe that God loves us and that he only wants to do us good all the days of our lives. *"For I know the thoughts that I think toward you, saith the LORD, thoughts of peace, and not of evil, to give you an expected end* (Jeremiah 29:11)." If you believe God loves you, then faith in his word will be easy. He may stretch your faith, but if you love him, and you know that God loves you, trust will automatically follow. God has given us his word. He has made promises to us. These are the things that he has planned for us before the foundation of the world. You cannot obtain these things by your own strength. They are supernatural and can only be obtained by faith. If you believe God, then do what he says and all of those things will come to pass for you. It is when we mediate on the promises of God, and when we strive with everything within us do what he says, that those promises come to pass. *"Whereby are given unto us exceeding great and precious promises: that by these ye might be partakers of the divine nature, having escaped the corruption that is in the world through lust* (2 Peter 1:4).*"* The lust (pressure) to conform to this world is ever with us, but when we renew our minds with what God says, we will be changed from the inside out. Babylon conditions men to lust after people and things for selfish gain. God wants us to come after him and his promises that transform the world with love. Babylon does not love. Babylon is about lust. Love is real. Lust is ever fleeting and never satisfied. These are two different roads of life with two distinct ends. One leads us to our *destiny in God* and the other leads to death.

Babylon **is** falling; its ways of achieving wealth, prosperity, power and great churches and great cities without God is gone **forever**. God's Kingdom is coming and His Will **will** be done in earth as it is in heaven. From the prophets of old, to Jesus Christ and the apostles, it has been said that God's Kingdom would be established in the earth. It will destroy all other kingdoms of this world; and God's Kingdom rule **will never** end (Daniel 2:44).

The Wine Of The Wrath Of Fornication

" For all nations have drunk of the wine of her fornication, and the kings of the earth have committed fornication with her . . . "
(Revelation 18:3)

In and of itself, there is nothing wrong with drinking wine. Jesus definitely proved it at the wedding feast at Cana, when he turned the water into wine. This was the first miracle of Jesus (John 2:1-11) recorded by the Apostle John. Even the Apostle Paul recommended to Timothy to take a bit of wine to cure a sour stomach (I Timothy 5:23), but the wine of the wrath of fornication is a different kind of wine. It has no miraculous healing power. Instead, it intoxicates men into doing abominable acts against God. It is referred to as the wine of God's wrath. Sin is like a cup of God's wrath being filled up as men continue in their sin. Babylon convinces men to follow her ways against God. This is spiritual fornication. The fruit of their evil ways will be stored up until the appointed time of God's wrath. Fornication is any kind of intimate relationship that deviates from God's design for humans. It can be either spiritual (apostate) or physical (sexual), or both. It always begins in the hearts of men who have turned away from God to form an unholy alliance with another. Once the heart is turned, the physical act of fornication will follow. Desires come from within the heart. Babylon places things before the eyes of men in an attempt to create a desire that causes one to depart from God. It is a lure that only works because of what is already in one's heart. A clean heart cannot be easily swayed, it will always desire to go after God and his righteous ways. That is why Jesus said to seek first the Kingdom of God and his righteousness (Matthew 6:33). By going after God, the things we need and desire will automatically come to us. Babylon tells us to go after people and things to find satisfaction. Men will then worship and serve the creation rather than the Creator (Romans 1:25). It always begins by turning the truth of God into a lie. This is the perversion that causes men to incur the wrath of God.

Blessed are those who hunger and thirst after righteousness, for they shall be satisfied with the everlasting goodness of God (Matthew 5:6). There are those who hunger and thirst for unrighteousness. For these children of disobedience, God gives the cup of his wrath. The pleasures of sin are only for a brief season. Remember, it is God who has designed this earth. This world was not created for sin. It was designed to perform the will of God in this earth. In these days of sexual freedom, people run to perform abominations as though life is an endless party. At God's appointed time, the party will end and someone will have to pay the bill. It's not that God is trying to break up our fun and hurt people. It's just how the original system was designed before the foundation of the world. Our times and seasons in this earth were ordained by God. These will not change as long as the earth exists (Genesis 8:22). It is also good to know that the penalty of sin is death. This was established in the Garden of Eden (Genesis 2:16-17). Also, if you take a person's life, your life will be required. *"Whoso sheddeth man's blood, by man shall his blood be shed: for in the image of God made he man* (Genesis 9:6).*"* These are the laws of the universe instituted by God. None of these can be changed or altered unless Jesus Christ is your advocate. These are things that Babylon knows, but refuses to tell you. Truth is bad for her business. It spoils all the fun of luring men into her trap that always leads to death. Let us consider the truth of fornication from the standpoint of the physical body. Since it is a perversion of the truth of God, we will call it *sexual perversion*.

When one thinks of sexual perversion the first think that comes to mind are those dark creepy individuals lurking behind closed doors lusting after another person they see on the Internet or in a magazine. You know the ones who leave their secret lairs and pounce upon women that they meet. We call them "perverts." They are called perverts because they don't seem to have the social mores to know how to keep their creepy lustful thoughts to themselves. According to God, this is a narrow definition of sexual perversion. *Perversion* is a corruption of something from its original state. In God's Kingdom, sexual perversion is anything of the sexual nature that is corrupted, or diminished in value from God's original purpose. What we see in our world, is sex that has been severely downgraded. What we call love is really *lust;* a zeal to covet or possess a thing or an individual for one's own selfish purposes. Lust is about taking, or stealing from another. Love gives freely of itself to another. In the absence of love, sex becomes nothing more than a lustful desire that will never be fulfilled. Lust leads to sin, and sin results in death (James 1:15). On the other hand, God is love, the kind of love that leads to a life of eternal fulfillment. That is eternal life; a life that is full of God himself; a love which never ceases, but forever satisfies the human soul.

When *lust* masquerades as love, perversion has manifested. For most of the world, this is the only kind of "love" people know, if they do not know God. Love is connected to the Blessing of God, which enriches the human soul without adding sorrow. Lust always brings sorrow. It brings what seems to be love for a short season, but once the thing desired is obtained, the "love" is gone. What one thought was love, was just an illusion. In fact, the illusion is the hook that lures one into fornication every time. Babylon always makes promises of love and satisfaction, but she cannot deliver what she does not possess. Only God can give those things, because they come from Him, for God is Love (I John 4:8). All Babylon can do is make the promise attractive enough to bait the hook. Once a person is hooked, she keeps then hooked with even more enticements, but the promise is never fulfilled. Babylon sells the **"gold of this world"** as the most desirable thing to possess. What is gold to God? He uses gold for pavement in heaven. What humans deem as valuable on earth, God uses like dirt and concrete in heaven. Humans are very limited in their earthly aspirations. We go after what we can see, which is why covetousness is such an evil. God looks beyond the shiny things like gold. He gives us vision of things not seen on earth. God's dreams are so big that lust could never compete. Lust looks on the outside to what one can see with the eyes, what one feels, or how one thinks. Lust goes for things that make us look and feel good about ourselves. It's a facade. It is an unobtainable image that is not real. What is real is **not** what we see in this world, but ***what is seen in the heavenly realm***; that which God places within the hearts of men. This true treasure; the Kingdom of God within man. God places it within us so we can make an even better world in which to live. It is how we bring forth even better things than what we see, and we bring them forth without sorrow.

In our day, the hot topic is gay marriage. People have been persecuting gays as if they are the only ones sinning against God. We all have. We continue to sin against God. When it comes to sexual sin, or sexual perversion, we all are guilty. It's not just about sex. It has more to do with the lack of understanding of the roles God created for men versus that for women. It has to do with not understanding why God created these bodies in his likeness and image. Why did God create sex anyway? If you don't know God's purpose for your lives, you will spend your time in perversion, trying to make it the truth. If you don't know what something was created for, you will abuse and misuse it. In the past, I have used the example of what happened when a family member came to visit over the holidays. We were all sitting at breakfast when one relative came down stairs talking about the fancy scrub brush that was in the shower. He put cleanser on it and bragged about how clean it got the shower. Someone politely informed him that it was not a scrub brush at all. It was a loofah which is used to rid the body of dead skin. This is the perfect example of how we abuse things if we don't know their purpose. Sexual perversion also stems from how men and women view each other, with and without a sexual relationship. The Babylonian way of thinking causes us to corrupt all of our most important relationships. If your car was not working right, you or your mechanic would have to open the manufacturer's manual of operation to see what is wrong. God manufactured these human machines and yet, few if any, actually open His manual (The Bible) to see why our relationships are not working right. Instead, people get divorced, or they find another lover and keep moving along their paths of destruction. There is no peace and there is no love. Of course not! Those things *come only* from God, who is love (I John 4:8). He is also the God of peace and harmony (Romans 15:33). If God is not in the center of your life, then he cannot be in the center of any of your relationships, so peace and harmony will elude you.

There will be those who still say, "it's only sex," or "it's only our bodies, so it doesn't matter." Really? Well, it may not matter to you, but it should. What you do with your body matters to God. Why would he sacrifice the body of his son on the cross if our bodies were not important to him? Why would the Bible say repeatedly to abstain from fornication and adultery if our bodies were not important? Why would God command his people not to marry outside of their faith? Why say do not be unequally yoked to a unbeliever (II Corinthians 6:14)? Why discourage people from having sex with a harlot or seductive woman (I Corinthians 6:15-16)? It's not because God is trying to spoil your fun. As a believer in Jesus Christ, we are members of his body. What we do with our bodies affects the entire Body of Christ. We are one with the Father, Son and Holy Ghost, in a spiritual marriage. Why would we join our Lord's body to a harlot? The devil has deceived both, the church and the world with sexual perversion. We are the temple of the Holy Spirit, who resides within us (I Corinthians 6:19). Why risk being cast out of the Kingdom because we have defiled the temple with sexual perversion? Repent! Be holy as the Lord is holy (I Peter 1:16). Babylon hates the ways of God. She uses lust to pressure people into sex and seduction of riches. This is how she lures men and women into her trap. Lust works because it appeals to one's pride. People like to be courted and complimented, but it is the flattery of evil lips that draws one into the snare (Proverbs 6:24). There is a reason Babylon is called the *"THE MOTHER OF HARLOTS AND ABOMINATIONS OF THE EARTH* (Revelation 17:5).*"* That is all she desires to produce. She hates God. She gets pleasure in using God's own people against him. That is why the Babylonian Church in America looks so much like the rest of the nation. Sexual perversion is rampant in the church. Christians have been openly criticizing gays, but they never deal with their own issues. If a single person has sexual issues, most leaders in the church will tell the person to get married. What happens now? That person uses marriage as a camouflage, while they continue seeing a lover, or continue viewing pornography on the computer. Like the world, these Christians would say that what done in private does not matter. Wrong! Jesus said that whatever someone does in secret will be uncovered. What is done in the dark, will be exposed in the light (Luke 12:2). If you are in the Body, you are in the Light. You are among the children of the Light. You cannot hide your sin. In truth, nothing is hidden from God (Hebrews 4:13). It may not come out immediately, but it **will** come out.

So, you say that you are not doing anything? Here is an example for you. There was a Christian woman who asked me to pray for her. God had promised her a husband and it had been ten years and no one had shown up. So, I prayed and the Lord gave me a prophetic word for this woman that I will never forget. He showed me that she had a sure word of prophecy about a husband. The Lord showed the man to me. He also showed me the garden of her heart at the time she first got the word about a husband. It was a beautiful garden filled with lush colorful flowers. Then the Lord showed me the garden of her heart on the day she asked me to pray for her. It was full of dead weeds. There was nothing living inside of her garden. Then Lord told me to tell her, ***"If you want your husband to come home to you, then let the other husbands go home to their wives."*** When I gave her this word, the woman swore that she was not sleeping with anybody's husband, but the Lord indicated that there were at least one or more relationships with married men that had to be severed if she wanted to get married. She was meeting after work for drinks with married men from her job. She said it was nothing, but when she stopped going out, one of the men became angry that he was being forced to go home to his wife. This woman had been deceived by Babylonian thinking that if you are not having sex, it is not an affair.

Fornication begins in the heart. The physical part is just a consummation of what was already going on between the two people. In this woman's case, it was enough to keep her from getting married. So many single women have asked me why they were not married and the answer was the same, you keep taking someone else's husband. Even if the man is not married at the time, you know he's not your husband, leave him alone. He belongs to someone else. Marriages are arranged in the spirit realm before they happen physically. God speaks a marriage in existence just like he does your prophetic destiny. Marriage **is part** of your destiny in God. Babylon says just pick someone and be happy. Well, they may be happy to a degree, but there will always be a *knowing* by at least one of the parties, that there is more for their lives.

Babylon tells people that marriage is about sex. That is just another Babylonian deception. It often trips people up when they learn the truth. Then they find themselves going outside of the marriage looking for another sex partner. Marriage is a God-ordained covenant. It is a lifelong commitment made before God, where each party promises to do their part in the relationship for the benefit of them both. The marriage covenant was mean to symbolize our relationship with God. The Bible even says that the man is the head of the woman just as Jesus is head of the church (Ephesians 5:23-27). Men are told to love their wives like Jesus loved the church. Jesus died on the cross for the church. He gave his very life for us, and yet men get married thinking that it is about women serving them. Jesus served the church by offering his body to death. Jesus showed his disciples how to love each other. He washed his disciples feet (John 13:15-17). This was the epitome of servanthood, and yet he was master of all. Babylon tells men to find a wife and make her your slave. It's a one-sided loveless way to live.

In God's Kingdom, you don't go looking for a wife. You seek your divine purpose and God will send you a *help meet* (Genesis 2:18) to do the work the Lord has called you to do. Some have use one particular scripture as justification for seeking a wife. *"Whoso findeth a wife findeth a good thing, and obtaineth favour of the LORD* (Proverbs 18:22)." This is a misinterpretation of scripture. This word *find* is not to seek. It means *to come by* or *happen to arrive at*. It implies that one is doing something else and the wife just appears. We don't go after spouses, God brings them to us when we are in our purpose. Adam was the example to follow. God put the man to work, and the wife just appeared on the scene. The Bible says that house and riches are the inheritance from our fathers (Proverbs 19:14). The prudent wife is from God. In our case, We get house, riches and spouse from God. He arranges it all for us. All things work together for our good, but only according to God's purpose (Romans 8:28). We've got this thing way out of order. Men are hunting down wives, and they aren't even qualified to be husbands. Until that man has a face-to-face encounter with God, he can't begin to understand what it means to be a husband. The same is true of a woman who wants to be a wife. *"Favour is deceitful, and beauty is vain: but a woman that feareth the LORD, she shall be praised* (Proverbs 31:30).*"*

Marriage is a serious thing for God. When marriage vows are made before God, there is a bond that is formed in the spirit realm. For those who are rooted in God, it will be a pleasurable bond, but for those where Satan has influenced their relationship, it may become a living hell. You cannot speak words before God saying one thing, and then act with your body and mind in the opposite direction, without invoking the curse. You cannot make such a vow and then say it was a mistake. Doing so may cause God to curse the work of your hands (Ecclesiastes 5:5-6). If you make a vow, stand by it. It was not a mistake when you spoke it, you just got weak when it came to upholding that vow. We mentioned earlier how the Lord said there were many abortionists in the church. These were the ones who took the word of his Kingdom and then aborted it. It would be better for them if they had never known the truth. Now, they have no excuse when they appear before the Lord. They cannot say they didn't know. All they can say is that they rejected that which God gave them.

In many ways, the American Church operates like a harlot, instead of the bride of Christ. Jesus did not enslave us, nor did he abuse us, and yet the church has chosen to leave what God offered, to create something of their own. They vowed to God with their mouths, confessing Jesus as their Lord, but they never let him lord over their lives. This is an adulterous relationship indeed. Where was the love? Where was the devotion to our Lord? If God's church is having relationship issues with him, why should we be surprised that America is having relationship issues him as well. The Lord blames the wicked, unfaithful men of God. They have not taken their vows before God seriously. If a man is not faithful to God, how could he be faithful to a wife and family? This infidelity flows from the leadership upon the congregation. It continues to flow from the congregation into individual families in our communities, to infect our cities, states, unto the nation and the world. Unfortunately, most of the world does whatever America does. We have been the blind leaders of the blind, as we pollute the world with our infidelities. The solution according to God begins with one man, just like it all began with Adam. That man is Jesus Christ, who came to earth to show us how to live. Do we listen? No! Human reason says that if you try harder, you can make it. If you are doing the same thing only doing even harder, that means you will get the same results even quicker. That is insanity. If you **want** something different, you must **do** something different. If you have been sowing corn, but you really want green beans, then you will have to plant seeds for green beans. Never will a corn seed turn into green beans. Again, lust will is never fulfilled, but sow seeds of unconditional love to get a harvest of love. This begins by loving God and obey him,. Once God shows you the purpose he has for your life, your whole perspective on life changes.

The Holy Spirit also gave me a word to speak on the subject of gay marriage. ***"Marriage in America is jacked up: it doesn't matter if it is a gay marriage or a heterosexual one; if God is not the center of your marriage, it will continue to be jacked up."*** In the eyes of God it doesn't matter if it is gay or heterosexual, if your marriage is not according to how he designed marriage, **neither** is pleasing in the sight of God. Now, this is not to say that God approves of the gay lifestyle. The Bible is quite clear on this matter, but what God **is** saying, is that we need to examine our own lives before stoning others. So what about gay marriages? The desire to get married is something that God puts within the hearts of people. God does not blame gays for wanting to marry. He says that they are looking for love anyway they can find it, but unfortunately because Christians have been so hateful towards gays, they have never heard that God is love. Christians have blocked the way for gays to receive what they are really looking for in this life. It's not sex, or a mate. They are looking for the love of God. In fact, most of the world that is seeking fulfillment, is seeking the love of God, they just don't know it. That which they are seeking can only come from God. When Christians block *the way* with their prejudices and hatred, this is a stumbling block that will keep people separated from the very thing they need. God is not freaking out because gays want to marry. However, he is very concerned that **his people** do not honor marriage. Not only is divorce rampant in the church; so is homosexuality, adultery and fornication. Pornography is also a big problem in many Christian marriages. An unbeliever cannot begin to comprehend the ways of God, nor should he be expected to. The things of God are spiritually discerned (I Corinthians 2:14). They are nonsense to those who are not connected to God by the Spirit. On the other hand, believers in Jesus Christ should be setting the example for the world to follow. People should see our good works and desire to come to our God, but this is not what is happening in America. There are some desperate souls coming into the kingdom, but the masses are still waiting for the church to be the witness God called them to be. The church needs to get out of Babylon, and show the world how the Kingdom operates.

Instead of pointing fingers at gays, take a look at what heterosexuals in the church are **still** doing, even after getting saved. They never gave up fornicating. They are thinking about it more than they are about God's will for their lives. They watch the same movies and listen to the same filthy songs that everybody else is listening to in America. Almost everything we see and hear in the media is filled with fornication and Babylonian thinking. Christians flock to this kind of entertainment and see nothing wrong with it. They have no clue that what they see and hear on a regular basis is programming their destiny. Instead of getting into the Bible and letting the Holy Spirit reveal God's vision for their lives, they are living out the vision of carnal men, who don't know God. People choose mates based upon the same "gold" standard. They look for the external things that fulfill the lusts of their eyes and their flesh. They care more about what someone looks like rather than knowing what's inside their heart. People are more concerned about someone's position in society and the type of education they hold, instead of finding out from God whether that person has the character and desire to be a good husband or wife. Would anyone buy a car that was beautiful on the outside, but the engine sputtered and backfired? Would you buy a pretty house because it was located in a impressive neighborhood, but the foundation was cracked and seeping water? No! A normal person would consider the investment of time and money involved in obtaining and maintaining damaged property, and walk away. So why is it that we don't do the same when considering a mate? Babylon has convinced the average American that it is better to be **with somebody** than to be alone. There are even some people who are addicted to crazy. They like the ups and downs of dysfunctional relationships. Again, these are those who have no clue that God has a good plan for their lives that involves peace and prosperity (Jeremiah 29:11). Babylon offers people glitz with no satisfaction. It is a curse. Only God can provide the Blessing, which brings abundant life and peace. The curse brings death, and yet God gives us a choice (Deuteronomy 30:19). Just know that if God is not in your marriage, Babylon is in control and the curse is in operation. That is why the divorce rate is so high, even among Christians. They have no peace and no harmony because God is not given first place in their relationships. Babylon believes that anything goes, and Christians are fornicating right along with her.

The Lord revealed to me that very few of **his people** actually marry according to **his purpose**. They most often choose a mate based upon desires of the flesh. They rarely marry the one God sends to them because there is an erroneous myth in the church concerning marriage. So many times I have heard people say that they chose a mate according to Psalm 37:4. Everyone who told me this, also misinterpreted this scripture. They told me that they believed that God would give them the desires of their heart. So, if they desired a certain person, God would give them that person. WRONG! First of all, that scripture says that God will give you the desires of your heart WHEN you delight yourself in God. When a person puts God first place in his or her life, then he places **his desires** within their heart. God's desires come from the invisible realm of the spirit. That is why the scriptures says that eyes have not seen, nor ears heard, neither has it entered into the hearts of men, the things that God has prepared for those who love him (I Corinthians 2:9). God's desires for our lives are revealed to our spirits by the Holy Spirit. Unlike, what Babylon and the American Dream tell us, we **cannot have** anything that we want in life. We **cannot do** what we want in this life. There are always consequences. They are built into this physical realm in which we live. The only safe things we can obtain without negative consequences, are those things which God has ordained for our lives. The human heart is easily deceived. According to scripture, *"The heart is deceitful above all things, and desperately wicked* (Jeremiah 17:9).*"*

When we delight ourselves in God, the focus is no longer on us, but our desire is to please God. Then the heart is ready to received the things that God has desired for our lives. Some how, we have the idea that God's desires are below our human standards of satisfaction. Not so! God created us. Don't you think that he knows best how to satisfy us in all things? He also loves us. God is not trying to spoil our fun. He is trying to protect us from harm while we have fun. God's desire is greater than anything we could ever ask or thing (Ephesians 3:20). When he places his desires within our hearts, it is all inclusive. It involves marriage, career and service to our fellow human beings. Remember that this is the Blessing which brings you into your wealthy place without sorrow. That is what God is offering every human on earth.

The spirit of Babylon lures men into believing that their way is better than God's way. Unbelievers are expected to follow Babylon. They don't know God. Now, for God's people following Babylon there are grave consequences. Jeremiah 17:5, says cursed is the man that departs from God to depend upon man's ways of doing things. Again, you may be saved from going to hell, but if you choose the curse, you will have hell on this earth. You will also be a poor witness for the Kingdom. The world is desperately in need of the Blessing, but the only ones who carry the Blessing are the Christians. If you carry the Blessing, but never manifest it in your life, what good are you to the Kingdom? You've become like the fig tree that Jesus cursed because it refused to produce fruit (Mark 11:12-14). The difference is that Jesus doesn't have to curse you. You chose the curse all on your own, when you decided to continue operating like Babylon. Now repent, and get back on God's purpose. Don't know your purpose? Then seek God with your whole heart in prayer and fasting, and find out what he has for you. Once you find your purpose, you will be less likely to hook up with just anyone in marriage. You will want to wait for God to send the right person; the one who is called to help you fulfill your purpose.

God chooses couples based on his purpose for their lives. Take a look at the first marriage recorded in the Bible; that of Adam and Eve. Adam was doing the will of God for his life when Eve was brought to him. The woman was created to be a helper (Genesis 2:18). She was designed to help Adam accomplish all God had designed for them to do on earth; and yes that including being fruitful, multiplying and replenishing the earth with more human beings. They didn't get married because of a desire of their own, but it was a desire that came from God. Adam didn't even know to desire a wife. What was a wife? That position was not defined until Eve showed up. Their marriage was not based upon sex either. It was not even in their thoughts until God placed it within them. Marriage was never to be based upon a human need. It was designed for God's purpose. Some might call this design, drab or boring, but it was a noble purpose. Marriage is very important to God. Notice that he didn't create a church or a religious organization at creation. God created a family. His desire was to have a family in this earth, not just any family, but one that was from God's direct lineage. This was the race that was to populate the earth. God chose Adam and Eve as the first family, the parents of all generations of the earth. It was a noble calling indeed. So it is for every family that has been set in this earth. We have a noble calling to populate the earth with a godly seed. It's not about the man and woman. It's about their seed, not just their children, but their children's children for generations to come. In fact, when God sees a man and woman in marriage, he doesn't just see their seed, but he sees their generations and their effect on nations. For instance, the name Adam means mankind. Eve is named as the mother of all living humans (Genesis 3:20). We saw this with Abraham whose name meant the father of many nations (Genesis 17:5). When Jacob's wife Rebekah was carrying Esau and Jacob, the Lord said to her, *"Two nations are in thy womb, and two manner of people shall be separated from thy bowels; and the one people shall be stronger than the other people; and the elder shall serve the younger* (Genesis 25:23)*."* The Lord told Jeremiah, *"Before I formed thee in the belly, I knew thee; and before thou camest forth out of the womb I sanctified thee, and I ordained thee as prophet unto the nations* (Jeremiah 1:5)."

In the eyes of God, every child is born with a purpose. With Babylon, it's all about personal pleasure and personal profit. Children in most cases are considered dispensable and inconvenient. Look at the family court systems in our nation where children are being used as pawns in divorce cases. The parents don't care about the children, only about how to use the kids to get at the other spouse. Even in our age of *sexual freedom*, kids don't matter. That is why abortion is so popular in America and around the world. People are even selling children for profit with no remorse. That is why record numbers of children are being trafficked as sex workers. Children have little or no value in Babylonian society, except they be used as harlots. If each generation produces after its own kind, what will future generations produce? What can harlots produce, but more harlots who are even more dispensable as men become more perverse and more violent. Even today, it's not enough to have sex with children, but adults are mutilating, maiming and killing these children deliberately in sex acts. This is Babylon.

That is how it was under the leadership of Nimrod. We learned that he terrorized men and led them to rebel against God. Where did this spirit come from? Remember that Nimrod was from the perverted lineage of Canaan, Noah's grandson. Even Noah's family did not escape the perversion of his age. In Noah's day, sexual perversion and violence was prevalent. Wickedness was great and the thoughts of men's hearts were continuously evil (Genesis 6:5). That is why God destroyed the world with the flood. Here is where the world is heading Jesus returns. Jesus said, *"But as the days of Noe were, so shall also the coming of the Son of man be. For as in the days that were before the flood, there were eating and drinking, marrying and giving in marriage, unto the day that Noe entered into the ark, and knew not until the flood came, and took them all away; so shall also the coming of the Son of man be* (Matthew 24:37-39).*"* In other words, Jesus is saying that before he returns to earth, people will be as corrupt as they were during Noah's day. They cannot get any better because Babylon can only produce the curse. A curse is a deterioration, or corruption of life that continues until either it dies naturally, or until God destroys the earth like he did in Noah's day. There will be destruction of this earth. People complain about global warming. They ought to read the Bible. This earth is destined to be destroyed by fire (II Peter 3:10). Therefore, global warning is just a glimpse of things to come, and the end is coming quickly.

This Babylonian way of life is on a course of destruction that cannot be stopped. There is only one refuge, that is in the Kingdom of God. Which is why God's people need to get out of Babylon and into the Kingdom before it's too late. If the people of God are destroyed, who will show the way to the Kingdom? God wants to make a difference between his people and the people of the world, but Babylon has captured the hearts and imagination of so many Christians that it is almost impossible to reach them. They have been deceived by religion. God's people have seen religion and they know that it is not the answer. The deception comes from the fact that Christianity is not a religion. It is a relationship with God and his son Jesus Christ. Religion kills the human soul. Jesus said, *"Come unto me, all ye that labour and are heavy laden, and I will give you rest. Take my yoke upon you, and learn of me; for I am meek and lowly in heart: and ye shall find rest unto your souls. For my yoke is easy, and my burden is light* (Matthew 11:28-30).*"* Religion burdens the human soul. A relationship with Jesus lightens your load because you are resting in what He has already done. Therefore you are not worried about anything, because he gave us another comforter in the Holy Ghost (John 14:16-17). Lust always lies to us. It tells us that we desperately need something that we really don't want or need. When we get it, there is no satisfaction, but it doesn't stop us from lusting. It's an addictive cycle of dissatisfaction. There is no peace anywhere to be found. It is a distraction that Satan places before us, to keep us from focusing on the precious and valuable things of life; our purpose and destiny in God. That is the treasure we all seek, whether or not we know it at the time. This treasure can only be obtained when you stop the madness of lusting after needless things, and turn your hearts to what God has already allotted for your enjoyment in this life.

Spend time talking to God and you will find yourself so full that there won't be anything that could lure you away from him. God is so big. His thoughts and his ways are magnitudes beyond our human imaginations. What he has for each of us is gigantic. People look to marriage as a way to complete their lives. God sees marriage as two complete people coming together to take on the impossible things of this world. Imagine two major corporations merging into one profitable organization and working towards a common goal. That is how God sees marriage. It is the marriage of two purposes into one gigantic purpose that is bigger than either party alone. The two become one colossal entity. This was God's plan for man before the foundation of the world. This was not just a plan for Adam and Eve, but for every person born on this earth. The Blessing of God is attached to our purpose. When we are out of God's purpose, we are operating according to Satan's plan for our lives. Satan wants to keep every human under his control. He also wants to keep them ignorant about who God created them to be in this earth. You see, Satan saw Adam and Eve, up close and personal. He saw the power and the glory that God gave them. There was glory emanating from their human bodies. They were the embodiment of perfection, even more perfect than how God had created Lucifer. *"What is man, that thou art mindful of him? and the son of man, that thou visitest him (Psalm 8:4)?"* Unlike the angels, these humans were created in the image and likeness of God. They were exactly like God in every way, but they had no comprehension of what that meant in this world. Likewise, Christians today have little or no comprehension of what it means to be filled with the fullness of Christ (Ephesians 3:19). We are ordained to be conformed to the image of Christ (Romans 8:29). That is the purpose for which God has predestined each of us, but it does not happen automatically. It requires that we make a choice to do things God's way, no matter what the world around us is doing. We have to put on the new man and walk in that way. Once God tells you who you are in him, you will look at life and at people in a whole new light. Then you will know that your body, your mind, your spirit are important to God. You will also find out that every thought you think, every word you speak, every action you take will either lead you towards or away from your destiny in God.

People with destiny in mind, lead very deliberate lives. Their mind is on the goal. They won't dare sleep around or degrade themselves in pornography. People with destiny in mind won't consider abusing or aborting their seed. They will begin to see life as God sees it. They will understand that a child carries his parent's destiny to the ends of time. A good man leaves an inheritances for his children's children (Proverbs 13:22), so does a bad man. One leaves wealth and the Blessing, while the other leaves poverty and the curse. One leaves a life of distinction, while the other leaves harlotry and shame. The good news is that God is always beckoning us to come to him, no matter what we have done with our lives. It doesn't matter how far you have gone, you are never too far that God cannot extend his arm to rescue you. You may even be in a gay marriage and sense all the negative pressure to conform to what the world wants you to be. Give all that up. Come to God. No one can truly change without surrendering to God. Let him love you the way you were created to be loved. It will transform your entire life.

Love has a way of transforming the way people feel about themselves. That is why so many people are always searching for someone to love. Guess what? It was God who started all of this loving going on. God is love. He created us in his likeness and image. We were created to love, not just other humans, but first and foremost we were created to love God. This is our greatest command (Matthew 22:37). To return to the true love (God), one must become like a child. Children rely on their parents for everything in this life. They constantly seek the approval of those who care for them. It is the act of caring and loving that causes children to reciprocate love. Children know they are not capable of doing what grown ups do. So, they tend to believe whatever the adults tell them. They trust their parents, even evil parents. Now imagine God, a loving Father who wants to provide every good thing for his kids on earth. We love him because he first loved us and gave his son for us (I John 4:19). Aren't you just a little bit curious about what Jesus died to give you personally? Wouldn't you like to see what inheritance God has laid up for you? Your earthly father may not have had the world's goods to give you, but God owns everything (Psalm 24:1). He is waiting to give it to whomever will come to him in faith, believing that *"No good thing will He withhold from those who walk uprightly* (Psalm 84:11)." If it is a good husband or a good wife (Proverbs 18:22), God has one for you. If is a good job or career position (Psalm 75:6), he has that for you too. If Babylon being evil gives good gifts to her harlot children, how much more would God give good gifts to his children. *"Ask of me, and I shall give thee the heathen for thine inheritance, and the uttermost parts of the earth for thy possession* (Psalm 2:8)." We don't have to belittle ourselves with demons or sell our souls and bodies in harlotry to be loved by God. All we have to do is come to him, and ask for what is rightfully ours as Children of God. Of course, we have to come the right way. No one can come to God except they go through Jesus, *The Way, The Truth and The Life* (John 14:6). Give your life to him today. Step through that Door of life. You will be forever changed, and on your way to new life which God ordained for you before the foundation of the world.

The Deceitfulness Of Riches

"... The merchants of the earth are waxed rich through the abundance of her delicacies (Revelation 18:3)."

One of the most dominant characteristics of the Babylonian spirit, is its allure in commerce and finance. In our modern world, everything is bottom-line oriented. It's all about making a profit. There is nothing wrong with that, <u>except</u> that the Bible says that it is the Lord that teaches us to profit (Isaiah 48:17). By His Spirit, God will lead us to our wealthy place (Psalm 66:12). It is God that gives us the power to get wealth (Deuteronomy 8:18), and yet people still chase riches and get rich quick schemes more than ever. We said that Babylon has people worshipping and serving the creation more than the Creator. God's Kingdom system is much easier. Things come to us when we follow God (Deuteronomy 28:1). The Babylonian system places people on a treadmill of toil with a promise of riches. Toiling for a living is the curse God placed upon Adam for sinning in the garden (Genesis 3:19). Jesus came to deliver us from toiling (Matthew 11:28-30), to place us into a life of believing God's word and receiving (Mark 11:24) what we need and desire.

Another outstanding thing to note about Babylon is the quality of merchandise that she sold to make the merchants and kings rich, *"The merchandise of god, and silver, and precious stones, and of pearls, and fine linen, and purple, and silk, and scarlet, and all thyine wood, and all manner vessels of ivory, and all manner vessels of most precious wood, and of brass, and iron, and marble, and cinnamon, and odours, and ointments, and frankincense, and wine, and oil, and fine flour: and wheat, and beasts, and sheep, and horses, and chariots, and slaves, and souls of men* (Revelation 18:12-13)." Where did Babylon get these goods? How did she acquire them? The Bible does not say for sure, but it sounds quite a bit like trafficking, and illegal trade. We also know that she was into witchcraft and enchantment with drugs (Revelation 18:23). Even if she stole the goods from others, the Bible makes one thing perfectly clear, every thing in this earth belongs to God. *"The earth is the Lord's, and the fullness thereof; the earth and they that dwell therein* (Psalm 24:1)." So, everything that Babylon has in her possession, actually belongs to God.

The Babylonian way of commerce in the world is grossly opposite of what God desires. The Babylonian Church in America has not fared any better. In the church we have seen the most extreme Babylonian views on money and wealth. Keep in mind that the Bible says that God is the one that teaches us to profit. He is the one who leads us to that wealthy place in him. So, why would prosperity preachers lure congregations into chasing after money and possessions? Why would others teach that money was evil, and encourage others to shun those who have wealth? Both camps were able to persuade multitudes of Christians by using Bible scripture to support their positions, but both sides are wrong. These ideas about money were taken out of Biblical context. It would take an entire course series to delve into the specifics of how these ideas continue to place God's people in bondage. For example, the poor are suffering. One camp says that poverty is God's will for their lives. Another says that the poor don't have enough faith, because God wants them rich. Depending upon which side is teaching them, God's people are confused about wealth and money. This was never God's plan for his people. At some point in history, the church began to confuse the American Dream with the Promises of God. That confusion is deeply entrenched in the prosperity camp. So, what is the truth? Is money evil? Does God want us rich? Is it true that God wants to give us the desires of our hearts; that he wants us to be happy? What about those preaching about supernatural money coming to the Body of Christ? It that for real? These are just some of the issues that have divided the church and have set them against the plan of God for money and finance in the Kingdom. There is also a racial component to the issue of money in the church. We will address all these issues in this chapter.

America was supposed to be the land which was overseen and watered by God himself (Deuteronomy 11:10-12). It was to be a supernatural lifestyle based upon our obedience to the Spirit of God. God had planned for us to have days of heaven upon this earth. So what happened? Humans decided to create their own Eden. We had the mistaken belief that our thoughts and ways are much higher than God's. As a result, we have always fallen short of God's plan for our lives. We wanted the riches. We wanted the goods. We just didn't want to get them God's way. Many in the church began following the American Dream because they felt it was easier than following after the promises of God. Others in the church denied money and riches altogether. While other committed themselves to thievery. When America began taking God out of the public square, Christian leaders also took God out of their congregations. Churches became *seeker friendly*. It was no longer politically correct to uphold the word of God. It also had a negative effect on offering collection plates. No one wanted to offend visitors to their churches. Consequently pastors and leaders allowed congregations to democratically decide what should be taught from the pulpit. Just like Americans at large, congregations began to have ears itching to hear what they wanted to hear. Even today, speaking the Biblical truth is not tolerated in many Christians churches. When prosperity leaders of the church began teaching about money, it sent congregations into turmoil. It should have been a relief from the decades of churches being in poverty and being told that money was evil, but it was seen as heresy. Men simply did not understand how God's Kingdom operated. They still don't understand today. In the past, if they didn't understand something, they just made up doctrine based on human reasoning. In their minds, if God did not manifest a miracle, it meant that God wants his people sick and poor as a punishment for doing evil. Some even believe that the supernatural power was only available for the first twelve apostles. They don't believe God moves in the same way today. Mention that God wants you rich, and you will be labeled a heretic for sure.

Why did God gave the initial revelation of money coming to the Body of Christ in the first place? God would have never spoken that word by his Spirit for no reason. He always speaks for a specific purpose. It had to do with the wealth transfer that is happening in the earth. There is money was coming to restore the Kingdom of God in the earth. It is not about possessing material things and accumulating wealth for oneself. It is about having enough to support our families, communities, cities, states, the nation and those of this world. It is the fulfillment of the promise of Abraham that his seed would bless the families of the earth (Genesis 22:18). Everywhere we turn there is a need, and God wants his people to fulfill that need just like Jesus did. But, you need money and resources to be able to fulfill all the needs of this world. And, you cannot give, what you have not received. So, if the church rejects the message of wealth and money, then it cannot receive wealth or money to do the will of God in the earth. They confused the message of the Kingdom with that of the American Dream. The Kingdom is about sharing with others. The American Dream is about accumulating for one's self. For the believer, we must seek God and his ways of doing things before wealth will be released to us. Many in the church went after material possessions, not having any clue about God's Kingdom agenda. This is the Babylonian way of doing things. Babylon goes after material things. We are commanded to go after God, and the <u>material things will come to us</u> (Matthew 6:33). Instead of doing things God's way, men have built their own kingdoms and have taken the glory away from God. We also saw this as people pursued the American Dream. People went after education, jobs, money, and possessions. It was all about each person accomplishing their own dream in lieu of following what God had planned for them since the foundation of the world.

The self-centered American attitude grew worse in the church when God's people went after riches. They began to have hatred towards the poor. Since the Bible said that poverty was a curse, poor people were treated like outcasts who were eternally cursed. If you didn't have plenty of money, they would say you had no faith. There was little help offered to the poor. In many cases, poor people were ostracized. Pastors began preaching that **all** that poor people needed was the word. That was not what Jesus taught. Neither was that what the first apostles practiced. Jesus taught the apostles to have compassion on the poor. In fact, in the early church it was common for people to sell their possessions and lay the proceeds at the feet of the apostles. The money laid at their feet was used to distribute to the poor so that none of them would suffer lack (Acts 4:32-37). In our day, money is being laid down at the apostle's feet, but very little if any is distributed to the poor in the congregation. People are being taught to give to the apostles, but there is nothing said about the administration of those funds to the poor among them so that none is in lack.

One of my favorite stories is told by the Apostle Paul in Galatians Chapter 2. His personal testimony is very similar to how God called me into the apostleship. Paul was called apart from the twelve original apostles. He experienced the resurrection of Jesus Christ by revelation (Acts 9:1-22). He met the Lord in a vision and that is where he received his call. Several years later, he met with Peter, James and John to reveal what the Lord had given him to preach to the gentiles. They were so pleased to hear his testimony that they gave him the right hand of fellowship. The apostles had only one piece of advice for Paul, and that was for him to remember the poor (Galatians 2:10). It was a common practice of the apostles to minister to the poor saints at Jerusalem (Romans 15:26). The Apostle Paul was so serious about ministering to the poor saints that he talked about it often in his writings to the churches. The most notable of these writings can be found in II Corinthians chapters 8 and 9. Preachers often quote from these writings, but few if any ever preach the complete message that Paul gave to the churches. First of all, Paul wrote about the grace of God given to the Macedonian churches who gave a generous financial gift even though they were in poverty (II Corinthians 8:1-15). Out of their love and concern for others, they gave **what** they had liberally, but not of their own. They gave themselves to God first, and gave as the Lord moved them to give. Paul mentioned their example to encourage us to do the same. Paul also talked about how Jesus came to earth and became poor so that we could become rich. Preachers often preach that it is God's will for his people to be rich, but that this was not Paul's purpose in mentioning what Jesus did for us. The Apostle Paul was using Jesus' example of giving his all, as an example for the church to follow. If Jesus gave up all he had in heaven so that we could gain the riches of the Kingdom, then we should be willing to give to our brethren in like manner. God is not asking that we go into poverty while helping the brethren. Paul spoke about *"equality."* He explained that the abundance of one saint should be used to supply another's lack, and those who lack in one area would use their abundance in another area to give their brethren.

We are the Body of Christ. We are not like the world that gathers material possessions to glorify themselves. We are called to love God and to love our neighbor. That is done through our good deeds and our sacrificial giving. In fact, these verses about the brethren taking care of each other's needs follows very closely with what Paul wrote to the churches in Ephesus. He told them that the church is a whole body fitly joined together and compacted by that which every joint supplies (Ephesians 4:16). We are the Body of Christ. There is no lack in Christ; therefore there should be no lack in His Body. If any member **does** lacks, it is because someone is out of order in the Body. There has to be unity "equality" in the Body of Christ. The early church was in *"one accord* (Acts 1:14; 2:1; 5:12)." This body of believers were *"of one heart and one soul* (Acts 4:32)." That is why the early church could sell what they had to help others. If the human body works together and heals itself, why is it so hard to believe that the Body of Christ can do the same to heal whatever is lacking? God is not asking us to give away all of our possessions. This also does not mean that God does not want his people rich? No! What God is saying, is that riches have a Kingdom mandate that gives glory to God. Also, not everyone in the Kingdom will become wealthy. First of all, the Lord told me that not everyone is called to have substantial wealth. The wealth and riches are appointed according to our assignments. Some people need little, while others with significantly larger assignments will need substantially more. Not all those who are appointed to great wealth, will actually receive it because they don't have faith enough to believe that God would provide it for them. Consequently, the Lord has only a remnant of believers who will receive and walk in their wealthy place on this earth. The Lord is also bringing into the Kingdom some new believers who already have wealth and who understand the purpose for money. They were just looking for the right cause to support. They will cheerfully give to Kingdom causes.

Wealth and riches have a Kingdom mission which is far beyond the needs of the individual. It's about the needs of the Body and about re-establishing God's Kingdom here on earth. I want to go back to the writing of the Apostle Paul to emphasize another money issue the Lord brought to my attention. There is quite a bit of controversy, at least in the word of faith camp, about giving to the poor. The Lord keeps bringing me back to this point, so I will take up where he is leading me. The same preachers who talk against the poor, often use one of the following scriptures to encourage people to put more in the offering plates. *"He which soweth sparingly shall reap also sparingly; and he which soweth bountifully shall reap also bountifully."* **Or**, *"Every man according as he purposeth in his heart, so let him give; not grudgingly, or of necessity; for God loveth a cheerful giver."* **Or**, *"And, God is able to make all grace abound toward you; that ye, always having all sufficiency in all things, may abound to every good work:* (II Corinthians 9:6,7,8).*"* These are probably the most popular offering scriptures used in the church. On their own, theses scriptures are powerful, but looking at the entire text from which they are taken, they are even more powerful.

The Apostle Paul writes beginning at II Corinthians 9:1, *"For as touching the ministering to the saints, it is superfluous for me to write to you."* Whoa! Did I read that right? This entire chapter was not dedicated to just any old offering, but one **for the poor saints**. He also called it *superfluous* to talk about giving to the poor saints? Obviously, it was very common to take care of the poor saints in the early church. The Jews set aside the tithe for the Levite (priest), the fatherless, the widow and the stranger among them (Deuteronomy 26:12). This type of giving was to remind them of where they came from. It was an act of thanksgiving for how the Lord had abundantly blessed them. The Bible is filled with scriptures that talk about the Blessing associated with taking care of the poor. How did some churches decide that the poor should be shunned? I don't know, but the Lord is not pleased with this practice. I have witnessed some rather despicable acts against the poor. Even the poor who tithe are mistreated. There have been church members told that they could only get financial assistance if they had paid <u>enough</u> in tithes. There comes to mind, two faithful couples who both lost their homes due to fire. They lost everything, and the insurance coverage was minimal. Their churches turned them away. I even recall a couple of Christian women traveling from Africa, who were stranded in this country due to civil war. The churches refused to help them. Instead, they were sent to the welfare office. What happened to taking care of the widow, the fatherless and the stranger? This should be one of the first priorities of a pastor for his congregation.

The unemployed poor are also mistreated. God never commanded his people to go out and seek jobs like the world does. This is how Babylon operates. In the Kingdom, if we have a need, we seek first the Kingdom. When we seek God, he will give specific instructions on how to get our needs met. He takes care of our need according to his riches in glory (Philippians 4:19). Now preachers will preach that God will take care of your need, but in practice they will tell the poor to go out and get a job. This reinforces what Babylon claims to be true; that world is a better provider than God. If God is such a great provider, why are his people coming to the world to get their needs met? The reason is simple. Preachers don't understand how God's Kingdom works, so by default, they do what the world does. Preachers also tell people that if they don't work, they don't eat, and sends them back out in the world looking for a job? Others are sent to the local welfare office. Instead of having pity on the poor as the Bible commands, preachers are putting the poor saints into more bondage to this Babylonian system of the world. If they are a member of the Body of Christ, then their main job is to seek God and obey him. Many of the poor who are sent away from the church will get a job and never return to God. Instead they become enslaved to the world's way of depending upon a paycheck either from the government or from an employer. It is the job of the church to disciple the poor and show them how God's system of sowing and reaping works, while helping them find out where God wants them to go for work. Otherwise, they will be lost to the Babylonian world and forsake the Kingdom of God. There is another side to this issue. Because pastors and leaders do not understand how the Kingdom works, they have placed a chasm between themselves and those who are called to work in the marketplace. There is an idea in the church that says if you are not called to full-time ministry in the church, you are not in ministry. This is simply not true. Jesus has commissioned the Body to go into all the world and preach the gospel (Mark 16:15). Some have preached that only apostles are called to go into the world. This is also not true. The commission to go into all the world was given **to all** those who believe (Mark 16:17). This means that for every believer that is working in the market place, he or she is there **on behalf of the Kingdom**. His or her job is not only to work at that place of employment, but also to demonstrate the Kingdom while on that job. God has called us ambassadors (II Corinthians 5:20) of the Kingdom. We are being sent to that employer, but we work for the Kingdom of God. This is not being taught in the churches. Therefore, many Christians are frustrated at their places of employment. It is one thing to be frustrated when God did not call you to that place, but it is quite another when God opened the door at that place and told you this was your assignment. If God called you to that place, **that is** your ministry. Again, seek God and his Kingdom plan for your life. He will tell you where you should be working. Everyone has a place in which to do the work of the ministry. It may be at home caring for children or the elderly. It may be in a medical or legal office, rather than in the pulpit of a church. No assignment is greater than the other. We are all members of the same Body. Each has a separate function, but all the members work together in unity to represent the Kingdom.

The Lord has sent to me to many of his leaders, at their place of employment. It became a normal thing to find out that they were the only Christian in the office. Some of them also had the worst attitudes towards their employer. So many Christians are frustrated working in a hostile worldly environment. They don't seem to understand the mandate to go into all the world and preach the gospel. The world is a hostile place. Jesus has to send us to them or they will be lost forever. In America, leaders are sidetracked by the Babylonian lust for money. Everyone, including church leaders look at employers as the source of income. No! **God is our source**. Therefore if someone is employed outside of the church building, he or she needs to know their place. First of all, did God call them to that employer, or did they come for the money or the prestige? If God didn't call them there, then they need to find out where God wants them to be. Secondly, what is their purpose for being on that job? What is the Kingdom mission? Answers to these questions can only be found by fasting and praying before the Lord. Church leaders need to think in terms of *deployment* instead of *employment.* Pastors should take care to see that these people are saved, filled with the Holy Ghost and sent forth as ambassadors for the Kingdom. Too little attention is placed on market place witnessing. It doesn't mean they need to beat their co-workers over the head with the Bible, or that they should be super-spiritual on the job. No! It means that they should be mindful of the fact that they are Kingdom citizens being deployed (just like a military peacekeeping force) into the hostile work world. They are not hired by an employer to get a paycheck. They are being deployed by the Kingdom to be an ambassador for Christ. They are expected to work for that employer, as unto God (Ephesians 6:5). Jesus never said Go ye into all the world and get a paycheck or a government check. He said go and preach the gospel. They will know you by your love (John 13:35). To send the poor to a worldly employer; or even to the welfare office, without this basic understanding of the gospel, is a discredit and dishonor to the Kingdom of God. It is also putting a severe financial strain on our federal government. People are hurting and God promises to bless those who care for the poor among them. The Bible says that a man who does not take care of his own poor is worse than an infidel (I Timothy 5:8). What would God say about a pastor, or a congregation that refuses to take care of their own poor? Selah.

This is more than just an issue about money or riches. It's about one's hearts. What are you thinking in your hearts about God? What you are thinking about your fellow man? The greatest commandment is that we love God above all. If we love God, then we will also love our neighbor (Matthew 22:37-40). Love gives (John 3:16). Again, this is a heart issue. We do all for the sake of God's Kingdom. Remember that the Kingdom of God is within us (Luke 17:21). The Holy Spirit deposits God's inheritance within our hearts. The entire plan and purpose for our lives is placed within our hearts at the moment we received Jesus as Lord and Savior. This is the Glory of God placed within our hearts; the treasure we hold in these earthen vessels (II Corinthians 4:6-7). That means that everything we need in this world, **is also** within us. That is why Jesus said to seek the Kingdom first. When we are deceived by money and riches, it is because we are seeking the world, and not that which God has placed inside of us. Our sole job in the Kingdom is to bring forth the treasure inside of us, and display it to the world. Remember Christ is us, the hope of glory (Colossians 1:27). People who are going after money, jobs and positions are those who are seeking after the world. Covetous people will not inherit the kingdom (I Corinthians 6:10). Additionally, hostility towards an employer will lock up that treasure. Love is the key that unlocks the treasure inside of you. Ask God where you need to be and what you need to be doing in this life. All the wealth you need is inside your heart waiting to be revealed.

Now, that we have that settled, let's take one final look at those offering scriptures the Apostle Paul wrote about. He said that those who give sparingly to the poor will reap sparingly. Likewise if they give bountifully to the poor, they will reap bountifully from the Lord. Again, we should give cheerfully to the poor according to what God has purposed <u>in our hearts</u>. Never give according to what you think, but according to what is in your heart. That is where the Blessing will be revealed. Only, after we have given to the poor in this manner, can we expect that the Lord to make all grace abound towards us so that we can always have all sufficiency in all things and may abound to every good work. The Spirit of the Lord told me that ***giving to the poor is evidence of our righteousness. Just like tithing, it is required of every believer***. Now, there are many who would argue with this, but I am not budging. I heard directly from heaven on this matter, and there is scripture to back it up. *"As it is written, He hath given to the poor; his righteousness remaineth forever* (II Corinthians 9:9)." Does this sound familiar? It comes directly from Psalm 112:9. In these last days, wealth will be coming to those who have a heart to give generously to the poor (Proverbs 28:8). This is a generational blessing. Don't take my word for it, read Psalm 112:1-3. The person who delights greatly in the Lord's commandment will do whatever the Lord requires; even tithing and giving to the poor. He does whatever it takes to honor God. This is not a person who is trying to get out of doing something. No! Honoring God, is this person's delight. If our hearts are not delighted in the Lord, it will be deceitful above all things and desperately wicked (Jeremiah 17:9). God wants to manifest his desires within our hearts, but it has to be a heart that is willing and obedient (Isaiah 1:19). God will show us the things that eyes have not seen and ears have not heard. Things that have never entered into the hearts of men. These are the things God has prepared for those who love him (I Corinthians 2:9). Let me give you a personal example. The Spirit of God began speaking to me about money and wealth in 1998. I was taking a sabbatical from the television and film industry. He set me aside to talk to me about things coming upon the earth; to give me a clear vision of my purpose in these last days. Although I had been a performer since I was a child, the Lord gave me a love for writing. For years, I had been toying with ideas for movie and television scripts along with movie scores, but when the Lord talked to me about money, he talked to me about writing books first. It began with a prophecy about a series of books I would write that would bring in ***"Millions, upon millions of dollars."*** This was the first time the Lord had even talked to me about money. This threw me off for a moment because I had been taught all throughout my church life that God didn't care about money. Here was God, talking to me about money. I could hardly believe what I was hearing. Then, the prophecy was confirmed by a local pastor, who told how God was going to spin off one of my children's series into film, games and more. He also mentioned the multi-million dollar success of these books. Okay. Now I knew that money was going to flow from my writings, **but** I still didn't understand why it was important to God. I knew there had to be a purpose for the money.

During this same time, I had ministry friends who were claiming that God was going to give them $50 million or more and big houses in Hollywood Hills. I remember asking them why they felt God would give them possessions for themselves, when none of those ministers were talking about plans for Kingdom projects. According to them, money was coming strictly for their personal use. Up until then, the only thing the Lord talked to me about were Kingdom projects. He talked to me about the nations of the world and all the things he wanted me to build; cities he wanted me to restore. I was so overwhelmed by this assignment, that I never even thought about asking about money for my personal use. My mind was preoccupied with trying to figure out where all the multiplied billions of dollars were coming from for me to complete what God gave me to do. On top of that, the Lord told me that this was just the beginning of what he wanted me to do. He also said that in these end times, money was coming to the Body of Christ to fulfill all the remaining assignments God wanted completed before Jesus returned. He wanted me to help the Body obtain their inheritances so we could finish the work. **Then**, Jesus could return. That made sense to me. My part would begin with the books the Lord would command me to write.

He explained that **just like he spoke a word and the worlds were created**, everything that was coming to me would begin with the word the Lord would give me to publish. These books would create endless income streams that would be used to fund the various projects, and create many companies that would fund even more Kingdom projects until Jesus returns. The Lord called it *"money with a mission."* Everyone was talking about money coming to them, but no one was talking about *money with a mission*. Then in 1999, there was a minister who came to Los Angeles by the name of Dr. Leroy Thompson. I had never heard of him, nor did I know what he taught, but the Lord had me go to his meeting. I heard this man repeat, almost word for word what the Lord had been teaching me about money and the purpose for wealth. This was all the confirmation I needed to step out in faith with whatever the Lord told me to write. <u>The Lord also had me sow seeds for all these things to come to pass in my life</u>. This is a wealth concept that few people talk about, but **in order to receive anything in God's Kingdom, you have to sow a seed**. You cannot get anything from God without first giving something. Most people think about sowing money, but you can also sow your time, gifts and talents or any natural substance to receive supernatural results. **Sow whatever God instructs you to sow**. Remember, its about the heart. The purpose is in your heart.

Most commonly, when preachers talk about sowing, they are talking about giving money. There is a practice within the word of faith camp called *"sowing upward."* It is common for preachers to tell you to sow into the life of someone whose has already made it. Others have preached that you should *"sow where you want to go."* In general, there is no problem doing this, **but** here is the issue I have with these practices. Men are looking at other men and they sow according to the accomplishments of men. If they like what they see, then they sow into the life of that minister. No! It's according to your faith. Your faith is actually the faith of God that is inside your heart. It's not your desire, but his desire for your life. We don't desire with our eyes, that is lust. In the Kingdom we desire with what God has placed within our hearts. The treasure inside of us must be revealed. If you can see it with your eyes, its not faith. It may be lust or covetousness, but it is definitely not faith. Faith is unseen with the human eyes. Don't look at men. Look to what God has placed within your heart.

Most people sow to the flesh; according to the lust or covetous nature, as men who want things. Sowing to the flesh reaps corruption (Galatians 6:8). This was one of the main issues I have encountered when working with pastors. They measure their success by the success of pastors. No longer were they looking to Jesus, the author and finisher of their faith. It was similar to the *animal pack mentality*. There is the perception that a particular leader is *"God's man."* All the other men strive to be like him; to dress like him; to drive what he drives and to live like he lives. No! No! No! God gave you a specific purpose. With that purpose comes an specific manner of dress and lifestyle. Let God tell you what belongs to you. I have known pastors who forfeited their own destinies to follow after another man. We are taught to esteem others more highly than ourselves, but disobedience to God's plan for your life is not acceptable. This is how most people sow their seed, according to the success of other men, and not according to what God told them to do. In doing so, they could be sowing **well below** the harvest potential God prepared for their own assignments. The Parable of the Sower (Mark 4:19) showed us that the deceitfulness of riches chokes and kills the word for your life. What has God spoken for your life? Don't let your eyes, or the lust of other things kill your promise from God. Stay in your lane. Keep your eyes on the prize that God set before you. That is the treasure in you that God wants to manifest in your life.

Don't sow to get what another preacher has. That limits God's ability to work his will in your life. The best practice is to **sow whatever, wherever and whenever God tells you to sow**. This is a prophetic word of instruction that will not return to God void. It will always accomplish what God desires (Isaiah 55:11) for you. For example, I was renting space from a corporation and they decided to increase the rent 22% without notice. My first response was to complain to God, "Why should I take money out of my ministry seed account to pay this man? My money is earmarked for Kingdom business." The Lord immediately responded, ***"This is Kingdom Business. You help this man pay off his building and I will pay off your buildings."*** I shut my mouth, thanked God for the word of wisdom, and I paid the increase. This was *sowing upward*, but only in the sense that this man had a building and mine had not yet been purchased. I had no intention of *sowing to go* where this man was going. He had the reputation of being a crook. He had even stolen some money from me. From the human vantage point, this did not look like good soil in which to sow a seed, and yet that is exactly what God had me do. God wanted me to help this man pay off one building, so that my future buildings in many cities, in many nations around the world would be paid for.

In recent years, the Lord had me reconnect with Apostle Leroy Thompson. I tuned in to his internet station and heard him talking about having people sow into his new Falcon 900 aircraft. The Lord gave me one word, *"Help him pay off his plane because you need a fleet of planes."* Again, my vision was not to get a plane like Apostle Thompson had. In my assignment, I needed <u>many planes</u> to be in operation <u>on several continents</u> simultaneously. People have been complaining about preachers buying luxury planes, but they haven't seen anything yet. The first aircraft the Lord told me to buy a Boeing 737. This would be the first aircraft in the fleet the Lord told me to build. It is a commercial airliner customized as a flying office/condominium. I didn't dream this up on my own. God spoke it to my heart. The buildings God wants me to acquire are far excessive, and well beyond anything I thought I would ever need. They are in God's plan for my life. He reminded me that my organizations will be working with heads of states around the world.

The Lord has been having me renew my mind even when it comes to buying houses. Whenever I found a house I really liked, God said I could not have it. Every house he said **was mine**, was massive in size and needed work. God and I were not seeing eye to eye, because I wanted small and comfort. A penthouse luxury hotel suite is all that I thought I needed, but God said no. In one particular city, he told me that my house was on a particular street. There were only a couple of houses that caught my eye, they were also old. I'd look where God told me to look, but then I kept a list of the ones I really liked in other areas. In a vision, the Lord showed how I was striving with him by looking at other areas. So, in my frustration, I said, "Cut me some slack here. There is nothing on this street, unless you know something I don't know." Bingo! Could it be possible that God actually knew something that Paula did not know? The Lord quickly gave me the address of the house. It was not on the market, but then two days later it appeared as a pocket listing with a very large multi-million dollar price tag on it. It too, needed work. It was obvious that they had begun a good thing, but the owner ran out of money and could not complete the work. Then the Lord told me that another house was mine. This looked good on the outside, but it had not been updated since the early 1900's. It needs total restoration. Now, the

Lord was showing me two houses. Each house cost nearly as much as an aircraft is to purchase and maintain. Then considering the work that needed to be done on these properties, it was started to weigh on me. Then God spoke a word that helped me renew my mind. He kept stressing the idea of ***"Restoration."*** Restoration takes work, but God said he had already placed the dream of restoring those houses in the minds of specific architects, artisans and designers. He reminded me that the Body of Christ would be working under a ***"Blank Check Anointing"*** until Jesus returns. Babylon tells us that resources are limited. In God's Kingdom, there are no limits. Just in these restoration projects alone, the Lord said I would employ hundreds of people whose lives will be sustained even if America's economy totally fails. These people will be taken off of the Babylonian system and placed in the Kingdom. These properties are not about Paula acquiring wealth. It is about putting the Kingdom flag of dominion in this earth and allowing God to use these properties as a platform (a pulpit of another kind) in which the Gospel of the Kingdom can be demonstrated before the world's very eyes.

I saw this so clearly while negotiating for the plane. I would be talking and all of a sudden I caught my self saying, "Amen!" When I spoke to the people about the hangars for my aviation department, "Amen" came up in my spirit. Before I got off the phone with the aircraft exec, he began talking about some of the faith-based projects they support in the various cities that they serve. Only God could have done this. When I got on the purpose God revealed to me, he was then able to touch the lives of everyone involved. Not only did God have to reveal what was mine. He clearly demonstrated that what he has for his people, is not even on the market. These are the treasures of darkness and riches hidden in secret places of the earth (Isaiah 45:3). Even with the plane God told me to buy. It was hidden from the masses. The Lord gave me very specific details about this plane. When first I enquired about such a plane, the aircraft people didn't even respond. Then I received an email from an aircraft executive in Switzerland, telling me to expect a call from one of their American counterparts here in the states. This man told me that what I was asking for, did not exist. He offered me other types of planes they had available, but none matched what the Lord told me about. The man asked me a bit about my company, and then he said, "There is one plane that has what you are looking for, but it's not on the market. It was customized by a certain billionaire. I know this plane personally. It's very nice. You would really like it. Let me make a few calls and get back to you." This is how I found my plane. God knew that billionaire's company was thinking about selling the corporate jet. He also had that billionaire design that plane exactly the way I needed. All that God has given me came from the unseen world around us. Babylon would have you look at what others have and covet to get them. God places things in your heart that are not seen, and tells you to call them forth in the earth. Flesh and blood did not reveal these treasures to me, my Father in heaven revealed it to my spirit. This is how Jesus built his church, not upon religion or upon the commandments and doctrines of men, but upon the revelation knowledge that comes directly from heaven (Matthew 16:17-19).

Whatever God revealed to my spirit was the *key of the Kingdom* that I needed to unlock the mystery of the treasure that the Holy Spirit placed in me at salvation. I called these things forth as the Lord directed. I sowed seed where he told me to sow, and then I sent out the harvesting angels to bring my treasures directly to me. Until those things showed up physically, I thanked God day and night for what he had given me. There was no doubt in my mind, that what the Lord showed me was clearly mine. Now, when you step out in faith like this, Babylon will still be talking and merchandising her wares all around you. Family, friends, even your pastor may be speaking what Babylon speaks, but you have to hold on to what God revealed and confirmed in your heart. You may even stir up the evil around you because all of heaven is in motion to bring forth your promise. No matter what that devil threatens against you, hold on to that promise and in due season you will be enjoying your harvest. The Lord has asked me, **"Paula, will you lead my people? Will you lead them to restore my Kingdom Dynasty in the earth?"** He spoke to me about the restoration of His ***Ancient Kingdom Dynasty*** in the earth. A dynasty is beyond the church that we know. It includes every industry and every facet of human life on earth. There are mountains of influence that God wants restored to his Kingdom. Up until now, the Body of Christ has been church-minded instead of Kingdom-minded. We have been deceived by riches and by the influence of the world, and we nearly missed the Kingdom plan of restoration. Now, I am hearing something so strong in my spirit, that I have to speak. God is in the process of placing **his people** in the ***"billionaire's circle."*** It's not about us. It's about **his plan** to go into the world. This is final stretch of the relay in the great commission that Jesus gave his church. We are at *"<u>**the end**</u> of the last days."* There is so much to be done, that the Lord has no choice, but to place the world's wealth in the hands of his people. This is what God is trying to get the church to understand, but if you are looking at the successful preachers as your goal, you have already missed God. People of God, stretch your faith and your obedience. God is about to drop the *"Father lode"* of wealth and power upon those who will honor him with their substance. Thank God for the remnant of believers who are willing and obedient to the call of taking back people and territory for the Kingdom. God has big plans for anyone who would yield to his plan and let his Spirit lead them to his perfect will. For those who think they have seen the best the world has to offer, you're right. This is **all** the world can offer, but the Kingdom of God is about to unleash some of the greatest inventions ever known to man. We are going produce luxury products that the world could never conceive. Those of us in the entertainment industry are about to unveil some of the most powerful productions ever to hit the box office. God knows what people want to see more than Hollywood ever could. God knows the needs of every heart, and he is about to prove it, big time!

The Spirit of God will supernaturally draw all men to God the Father, through every facet of our human existence. It will be God unleashed, in all of His Glory! If you want to be part of this Kingdom Restoration, don't go after riches. Don't go after influence. Go after God and his Kingdom plan for your life, and all of these things will be richly added to your life in abundance!

CONCLUSION

It's All About The Human Heart

"For within, out of the heart of men, proceed evil thoughts, adulteries, fornications, murders, thefts, covetousness, wickedness, deceit, lasciviousness, and evil eye, blasphemy, pride, foolishness: All these evil things come from within, and defile the man." Mark 7:21-23

When all is said and done, the Spirit of Babylon thrives because of what men have taken to their hearts. The church falls prey to this spirit because they do not understand their position in the Kingdom of God. Here is the issue. Babylon has become the habitation of devils (Revelation 18:2). This is where the demons live and thrive. Dear Christian, know ye not that you have been delivered from the power of darkness? Know ye not, that you were translated into the Kingdom of God's dear son (Colossians 1:13)? God did this because he loves you. He wants to reconcile you back into his family. God wants to give you an inheritance, but if you continue in darkness, your inheritance will be lost, just like it was with Adam. The first Adam was lord and ruler of all of this earth, but he esteemed his position lightly. Therefore he took heed to the voice of a demonized serpent instead of heeding the command of God. Adam fell because of the wickedness of his heart. He had little value for what God had given him, and placed more value on what the serpent said. Adam valued evil over good, and took it to heart. What a man takes within his heart becomes his treasure. When we choose evil over good, this is how we defile ourselves. When we see or hear evil and begin to imagine it in our hearts it's only a matter of time before it manifests in our lives. *"A good man out of the good treasure of the heart bringeth forth good things: and an evil man out of the evil treasure bringeth forth evil things* (Matthew 12:35)."

You are light, and no more darkness. What kind of communion can light have with darkness (II Corinthians 6:14)? God has given you exceeding great and precious promises (II Peter 1:4) to treasure in your heart and bring to pass, so that you can escape the darkness and corruption of this Babylonian world. These promises empower you to live like Jesus lives. As he is in heaven, so are we here in this world (I John 4:17) **if** we hold on to our faith. We should be walking and talking like sons of God in this earth. Instead, the church comes across as foolish as it walks in the wisdom of religious men; out of touch with both the world and the God whom they claim to love. The sons of God are those who are led by the Spirit of God (Romans 8:14). The sons of the devil are those who are led by the devil. Whomever you yield yourself to obey, is your master (Romans 6:16). As believers in Jesus Christ, you have a way of escape from the issues of this world. The Kingdom of God is within you (Luke 17:21). When you gave your life to Jesus Christ, the Holy Spirit came to live inside of your heart (II Corinthians 1:22). The Holy Spirit bears witness with our spirits, that we are the children (sons) of God, and joint heirs with Christ to all that God the Father has both in heaven and in earth (Romans 8:16-17). This is the inheritance God, which is reserved in heaven for us (I Peter 1:4). God has given the Holy Spirit as a guarantee that the promise we hope for, will indeed come to pass. What hope is that? Our living hope is that of bodily resurrection from the dead just like Jesus was raised from the dead. It's our faith in the resurrection that got us saved. Romans 10:9 says, *"If thou shalt confess with thy mouth the Lord Jesus, and shalt believe in thine heart that God hath raised him from the dead, thou shalt be saved."* Here is the really good news. We don't have to wait to die, before experiencing this resurrection power. If the Holy Spirit raised Jesus from the dead, he can also quicken your mortal body (Romans 8:11) and raise up every thing that is sick and dying in your life today. That is the kind of power that is living inside of your heart. You only have to activate it by your faith.

Christians are taught that coming to Jesus means forgiveness of sins and going to heaven. Although this is correct, it only the beginning of God's plan for salvation. Salvation is about *total restoration* back to God's original plan for our lives. God has given every believer a "ticket" to living days of heaven upon the earth. While the rest of the world is suffering and scrambling to make a living, God has given you an inheritance, the Blessing that will be fruitful and multiply the goodness of God in your life. It will replenish whatever is lacking, and cause you to live in dominion over the darkness of this world. So, why aren't we seeing this miraculous resurrection power working in the lives of everyday Christians? They have taken heed to the voice of Babylon over the voice of God. They are doing exactly what Adam did, and it is causing them to live in the curse. I asked the Lord many years ago, why his power was not manifesting through his people. In the spirit, he showed me a picture of the human heart. The Holy Spirit was in there, but it was being crowded out by other things such as family values, tradition, past hurts and pain, ignorance, religion, pride, fear, intellect, sorrow and grief.

These were the things that people treasured more than God's word. This is a form of idolatry. When we worship and esteem something or someone higher than we esteem our Creator God, this is idolatry. If this is your issue, then repent. Ask the Holy Spirit to help you get back in faith.

There are also those who think that God's way is too hard. It is a narrow way indeed (Matthew 7:14), but it is very possible to accomplish, if you let the Holy Spirit lead you. Why does it seem that it is easier to do evil than good? It has to do with momentum. Have you ever been in a crowd that was going in the same direction, and it felt like you were being pushed along the way? That's momentum. I was heading home after work one day. When, I got out of the subway station, I ran into a political demonstration. Hundreds of thousands of protesters had taken to the streets. I lived only a block away from the subway, but that day it took much time and effort to get home. Why? I was going in the opposite direction of the crowd. This is called resistance. The momentum of the crowd was going against me, but eventually I made it home. Operating in the spirit is much the same way. Since Adam sinned, the spiritual momentum of this world has been in the direction of the curse which leads to death. The Lord gave us the Holy Spirit, and a new way of living in the Blessing that leads to eternal live. In order to get there, you are going to have to go against the crowd, and keep walking until you obtain your promise. We must submit to God's way and resist the devil (James 4:7), resist the naysayers and haters to get what heaven has for us. If I had stopped walking when I was trying to get home, that crowd would have swept me in the opposite direction. I would have eventually wound up at another destination instead of where I wanted to go. The same is true in the realm of the spirit. If you do nothing, or if you stop holding on to your faith, you will automatically end up missing the promises of God. You have to make a conscience determined effort that you are going to move forward with what God said, no matter what the crowd is doing. You may have to resist all the negative comments from friends and family, even the negative thoughts in your own head. Open your mouth and speak what God promised. Cast down those evil imaginations. You have a promise to obtain. Remember what God told Joshua when he was about to sack Jericho? *"This book of the law shall not depart out of thy mouth; but thou shalt meditate therein day and night, that thou mayest observe to do according to all that is written therein: for then thou shalt make thy way prosperous, and then thou shalt have good success (Joshua 1:8)."*

Now, if you are a believer, living in the curse and the demons do not bother you. Something is wrong. You are far removed from God and his purpose for your life. Check your love walk. Are you holding something against another? Is there unforgiveness in your heart? Are you harboring unclean thoughts about yourself or others? If so, you will have no inheritance in God (Ephesians 5:5). Here is why. Your inheritance is in the Kingdom of God that is within you. We know that God is love, so let's call it the Kingdom of Love within us. In order for it to be released, you must give God (Love) first place in everything. Remember the Kingdom is your treasure in your earthen vessel (II Corinthians 4:7), but so are the secrets that defile your heart. You will either yield to love, or to the other because you cannot serve two masters (Luke 16:13). How can you tell which is your master? Look at the results of your life. Listen to the words of your mouth. Whatever is inside of the man will eventually come forth, either by what he says, or by what he does. *"For out of the abundance of the heart the mouth speaketh* (Matthew 12:34).*"* Whatever we give the most attention to in our hearts will also manifest the most in our lives. *"For with the same measure that ye mete withal it shall be measured to you again* (Luke 6:38).*"* That is why we are told to guard the heart with all diligence (Proverbs 4:23). This is the source of our lives. Everything we have in this life came from within our hearts.

Take a look at your life today. How many things in your life have happened just the way you heard or thought they would happen? If your mom or dad said you would always be a failure, were you indeed a failure? Why, or why not? Think about it. If it happened, it was because you believed what they said and meditated on it in your heart. Then you spoke it with your mouth. If it didn't happen it was because you believed something else, meditated on it and spoke those words with your mouth. We will have what we believe in our hearts. What we believe always comes out of our mouths, because our world is created by our words. And, we have what we say (Mark 11:23). This is how God created us, to be like him when he created the world (Genesis 1:3). This is how we get saved. This is also how we receive everything God has purposed for our lives. If you want what God has for you, then change what you are hearing, thinking and speaking. Replace it with the word of God. Hold on to that word. Meditate on it. Speak it with our mouth, then watch it come to pass. In due season, you shall reap, if you faint not (Galatians 6:9). God's word never fails.

Kingdoms May Fail, But God's Word Shall Prevail

Throughout the Bible, there is one consistent fact, *if God spoke a word concerning anything, then he will surely bring his word to pass.* Whatever God speaks **has** to come to pass. If God said that Babylon will fall in one day, it shall be so. Almighty God created this world. He set the times and seasons for our existence on earth (Acts 17:26). We did not create ourselves, nor did we set the universe in motion. Who do we think we are to exalt ourselves against the one who gave us our own breath? God knew each of us before we were formed in the womb (Jeremiah 1:5). He knows the end from the beginning (Isaiah 46:10). God's word will not return to him void, but it will accomplish what he desires and it will prosper in the thing where he sends it (Isaiah 55:11). Even with all the Biblical evidence of the infallibility of God's word, men (even religious men) always carry on, as if God is just a man who is prone to lies and deception. The word is clear, God is not a man that he should lie; nor is he the son of a man that he should repent (Numbers 23:19). Yet, God's people have an issue with believing his word.

People are hurting all over the world. God placed the solution inside the hearts of his people. There is nothing that we are experiencing on earth, that God had not seen coming. In fact, he also predetermined the best possible solution to cure whatever comes against us. Babylon tells us to look to the world's experts for solutions, but they are not there. God placed the solutions in the earth to be discovered by those who will seek him first. If the church does not believe God, how can we convince the rest of the world to follow him? The church has to get out of Babylon! Like the kings and merchants of the world, the church been bewitched by Babylon in the multitude of her sorceries, and the great abundance of her enchantments and spells (Isaiah 47:9). They are caught up with a demon they cannot see, nor do they recognize Babylon as a threat to their salvation. We see it throughout American life. People are going along with a program that leads to destruction, but you cannot tell them the truth. They don't want to hear it. Same is true in the Babylonian Christian church. If you attempt to tell them the truth, they will try to kill you. They don't want to change. They won't let God do what he wants to do in their lives because they are convinced that Babylon is the only way to live. Seeking God and his Kingdom first is not even a consideration.

Christians believe that Babylon and all of her educated experts have all the answers they need. What happens when Babylon falls completely? It is falling before our eyes and people are starting to panic. There is anger and violence in the air as people are scrambling to get their share of what they consider "limited" resources. This anger is exaggerated during election seasons. Instead of praying and asking God what to do, the church gets in the middle of the heated debates. This causes many to go against the will of God. The church takes sides with certain parties, but the answers are not in either party. The answers are in the Kingdom. You have to seek God to find them. We don't choose candidates based upon what they say, but based upon what God says. The church gets caught up in the witchcraft of the election process. I'll never forget what Lord showed me in the 2012 Presidential election. I was in prayer and all of a sudden, witches arose and stood like a mighty army around one particular candidate. It just so happened to be the same candidate that church leaders were telling congregations to support. Then the Lord showed this candidate going straight to hell, and all those prominent church leaders were willingly following right behind him. The devil was having a field day because the church was caught up in the witchcraft of Babylon and the God's leaders were taking the people straight into hell. Even when God places **his** person into office, the people of God don't realized that they should be praying for those in authority (I Timothy 2:1-2). Those politicians are dealing with spiritual battles they don't even understand. They need the church to pray, and yet like all ignorant Americans, Christians are speaking evil over the powers God has ordained for our good (Romans 13:1-4). God's people have been bewitched by Babylonian thinking. God wants to turn his people around, but they have to repent and get out of Babylon before it is too late.

The Bible says that when Babylon falls, all her calamities will come in one day (Isaiah 47:9), even in one hour shall her judgment come (Revelation 18:10). The world will see it and wail for her. The entire world will be paralyzed, as will be the church. What will happen to all the merchandise Babylon stole? That merchandise is about to be returned to the rightful owners, the people of God. This earth was created for the enjoyment of God's family. When Adam sinned, it was all stolen. Babylon has been peddling stolen goods since Adam fell. God's promise was that before Jesus returned, everything would be returned to his family; both the people and the possessions of this world. The Lord reminded me of a vision he gave me several years ago. It was about world domination. The Lord took me into his *War Room* where he showed me a map of the world under enemy occupation. He said that occupation began when Adam lost his place as ruler of this earth. The world, and Adam's position were taken over by satanic rule, and remained that way until Jesus restored the earth and its people for God's Kingdom. The Lord then drew my attention to another map of the world that was hanging on the wall. He said that the map on the wall was the legal document showing the earth and its territories as having been restored to God. The Lord said that everything that was restored, was **placed in receivership** for the Body of Christ to claim and manage until Jesus comes back to reign on earth.

When I took a closer look at the map on the wall, I noticed that there were family names attached to the land, to industries, and governments around the world. It reminded me of those ancient maps that described how the land was divided among the original tribes of Israel. The Lord explained that the entire earth was to be divided amongst all of his children. The Bible talks about Israel having a promised land, but God said that everyone who comes into the family through Jesus Christ, also has an inheritance in the land. There are some who teach that our inheritance is only spirit. That is not true. Our inheritance is both physical and spiritual. That is why we need to seek first the Kingdom and let the Lord reveal what belongs to us. Anytime I possess another piece of property, I stake a Kingdom flag to that property. I am reclaiming my part of what was put in receivership, but I am also letting the devil know that his occupation is definitely over in my life. Babylon, in her use of the American Dream, has duped the people of God into believing that all we need is a house, car and provision for our own family. No! No! No! **God wants us to Bless the families of the entire world** (Genesis 22:18). That is the Blessing of Abraham. This is the same Blessing that Adam had. This was also the same Blessing that God gave to Noah and his sons. The sons of Noah (Shem, Ham and Japheth) were suppose to spread that Blessing across the world. The only son that obeyed was Shem, but the Blessing was still appointed for Ham and Japheth. God never changed his mind about Blessing the world. Then God chose Abraham (descendant of Shem) and his seed to carry the Blessing to the world. The Jews came from the bloodline of Abraham, but they never spread the Blessing to the world. They got stuck in religion, and never possessed their land. God **had** to send Jesus, to get the Blessing to the world. Jesus Christ is the seed of Abraham (Galatians 3:13-16) through which the rest of the world (descendants of Ham and Japheth) can receive the Blessing. Now remember that the ancient Jews thought it was only about them. They believed that the Gentiles (non Jews) were unclean. Consequently, they made enemies of the very ones God wanted them to Bless. The message then was given to the first church that was formed days after the resurrection. Jesus left the command for them go into the world, *"But ye shall receive power, after that the Holy Ghost is come upon you: Ye shall be witnesses unto me both in Jerusalem, and in all Judaea, and in Samaria, and unto the uttermost part of the earth (Acts 1:8)."* Did they go as commanded? No! After the stoning of Stephen, the Lord allowed great persecution to come against the church, which caused them to scatter. *"And devout men carried Stephen to his burial, and made great lamentation over him. As for Saul, he made havoc of the church, entering into every house, and haling men and women committed them to prison. Therefore they that were scattered abroad went every where preaching the word (Acts 8:2-4)."*

Which brings us to the Babylonian Christian church in America. We followed after the pattern of the Jews. Although Jesus commanded that we go into all the world to Bless the world with the Gospel, the church refused to go. Instead they decided to support Israel. How can we help someone else receive from God, when we have never received what God gave us? American Christians are fighting for Israel's right to possess their land, but we have refused to take ownership of the land that God gave us. The Body of Christ has land to possess. According to God, he gave the land of America to the church, and they have yet to take dominion for the Kingdom. Freely we have been given this land, but never have we received. You cannot give what you have never received. The church in America never took ownership of this land, and yet the Lord says, **"What happens to America, depends upon the church,"**

Again, Babylon has duped the church into competing with the world. Remember how we said that Babylon entices competition for things she does not own, hoping to get the highest bid by fraud. The church was never called to compete. We are called to DOMINATE! **The earth is the Lord's and the fullness thereof. The earth and they that dwell therein.** Are we not heirs of God and joint heirs with Christ? Then all of this earth belongs to us. It is time for the church to take ownership. From the Christian view, this land is unclean, filthy and going to hell. Guess what! God knows what goes on in America. That is why the Lord placed the church here. He wants us to take dominion and clean America up. Instead, we act like grasshoppers running from the giants in the land. Yes, the sons of Anak are here, but so are the SONS OF GOD! We don't run away from the giants. We are called to slay the giants and possess the land. Yes, violence and terrorism will increase because the Anakins don't want to give up the land, but they have no choice. God has spoken and his word will come to pass, with or without the cooperation of the giants. Mind you, this will be a spiritual battle like none this earth has seen. The Spirit of God calls it *"The grande finale before Jesus returns."*

No one is really talking about taking ownership of this nation's condition, and yet God blames the church for America's current state. We never did what Jesus commanded us to do. We went to Africa. We went to India, but we refused to go into America. God had to send missionaries from other countries, to get this nation saved. So what will God do next, in order to get the Blessing to all of the world? He is going to bring a great storm to America that will cause the church to scatter. Here is how the Lord explained it to me, *"Instead of standing on the word and preaching against the wickedness of America, the church boarded a ship and headed to Israel."* The Lord said that he is about to, *"Overthrow the ship the church boarded to Israel, and he has prepared a great fish that will bring the church back to its righteous mind."* What about the *Tower of Religion* that the church built in America? The Babylonian church will cease in its function and the people will be scattered. Some will *fall away* from the faith because they were deceived by religion. Others will *fall into* their purpose and do what God called them to do. Out of this storm that is coming to America, King Jesus will raise up HIS CHURCH, one that is built upon the rock of revelation knowledge.

When the storm comes upon America, many will say that it happen because we didn't fight to support Israel and its border crisis. This is absolutely false. According to God, the border battle in Israel is a *political battle* that we must avoid. The church is called to be ambassadors, not a political organization. We lead by setting the example for the world to follow. Besides, human beings don't bring prophecy to pass, God does. *By interfering with Israel in its political issue, the Lord says that the church has created another Hagar situation for that nation.* You will remember that God told Abraham and Sarah that they would have a child in their old age. Sarah decided to help God bring the prophecy to pass, by offering Hagar her servant to Abraham to conceive a child. As a result, Ishmael was officially the first born son of Abraham, however God did not approve. The birthright was destined only for the child which Abraham and Sarah conceived with their own bodies. And when they did, Isaac was born. Since Abraham's day, there has been an ongoing battle between the seed of Ishmael and the seed of Isaac over the birthright. Today, the Lord is saying that the church has done the same. ***By taking Israel's side in this land battle, the church has made themselves enemies of the same Muslim countries that God intends to Bless***.

God is so serious in this matter concerning Israel that he commanded me to tell his people, ***"Leave Israel Alone."***[1] Here is what the Lord gave me to publish in my book entitled, **The War Journal (1999-2010) Volume II**. *"The church has created a cataclysmic conflict with God akin to when Jonah refused to go to Nineveh. Jonah didn't feel that Nineveh was worthy to be saved; so he got on a boat and headed to another city. Likewise, God has spoken to the church concerning the plight of the United States. Many have been given specific instructions for getting the country back on track. Instead, many pastors and leaders are packing up and heading for Israel . . . The Spirit of God says that this kind of support is being done by the church while ignoring the Biblical mandate to care for the poor, widows and fatherless within our borders first. The Spirit of God calls this disdain for the poor, Anti-American behavior."*[2] The Lord has identified an evil motive behind this support for Israel. He not only calls it rebellion, but he also calls it *"Anti-American behavior."* In Jonah's case, he did not think that Nineveh was worth saving either. In general, the leaders of the American church believe that our nation is condemn to be destroyed. After all, as some would say, "The Bible doesn't say anything about America, but it does tells us what is going to happen for Israel." Revelation 22 tells us that in heaven there will be many people from many nations and tribes. This verse alone proves that God has a plan for every nation on earth. No nation, including the United States has been left out of the plan of God. Even so, Jesus said that His Church would be built upon revelation knowledge. No one seems to care what heaven has to say. This is how the Babylonian Church arose. Religious men having no relationship or re-

1   Matthews, Paula. "Issues of Conflict."*The War Journal (1999-2010) Volume II*. Los Angeles: Spirit & Life Publications, 2010. 64. Print.
2   Matthews, Paula. "Preface."*The War Journal (1999-2010) Volume II*. Los Angeles: Spirit & Life Publications, 2010. 15. Print.

velatory knowledge from God, make decisions based upon their human intellect. This is what Babylon does since she alone has all the experts and seasoned counselors and advisors (Isaiah 47:10,13). This is wisdom of men and doctrine of devils. We have set up nations with a lie, telling them that God only judges them by how they treat Israel. Grant it, the Bible says touch not my anointed and do my prophets no harm (Psalm 105:15). That scripture applies not only to Israel, but to anyone who is in the Body of Christ, but let's take this a bit deeper.

Take the passages beginning with Matthew 25:31 that talk about what will happen when *every person from every nation* must appear before the judgment seat of Christ. How does Jesus judge them? *"For when I was an hungred, ye gave me meat: I was thirsty, and ye gave me drink: I was a stranger, and ye took me in: Naked, and ye clothed me: I was sick, and ye visited me: I was in prison, and ye came unto me* (Matthew 25:35-36).*"* When did we see Jesus in any of these conditions? If it wasn't Jesus, who was he referring to in this passage? *"Inasmuch as ye have done it unto one of the least of these my brethren, ye have done it unto me* (Matthew 25:40).*"* Who are the brethren? The saints of God, the Body of Christ. Jesus will judge each of us according to how we have ministered to the poor and suffering saints in the church. The Lord keeps bringing me back to this point, because Babylonian church leaders have taught that we should only support Israel and not poor Christians in our nation. Instead, we have sent the poor to the government to support, while sending millions of dollars to support the poor in Israel. If we don't support our own poor in America, the church is worse than an infidel (I Timothy 5:8). I've heard so many preachers preach, if you don't work, you don't eat. Did Jesus ever say this to the poor in the church? Did the apostles? No. So, why does the church say it? They want to get out of their responsibility of taking care of the poor. Again, I hear it echoing in my spirit, these words, **"There is no lack of resources, only a lack of obedient people who are willing to share their time and resources with others. And, when we refuse to obey God, we curse ourselves."**

There are pastors and leaders whom God has called, that are suffering financially. Their parent ministries refuse to help them. No one is teaching them how to live by faith. These mighty warriors are not in cushy offices and plush churches. They are on the frontline battling the war on poverty for the masses. They are giving all they have to the people they serve. They are doing the work Jesus did, but have yet to see the miracles that brought in the money and multiplied the bread and loaves. Then there are the wealthy churches that are hesitant about helping the poor. Pastors at my home church were complaining that there were too many poor, that the staff stop helping them. I was told by one pastor, "I don't know how to deal with **those** people." "**Those** people,"are **God's** people. Where was the pastor's faith? Where was the Blessing that multiplies and replenishes what's needed in the earth? If they would have just stopped to seek first the Kingdom and let the Lord speak to them, they would have known how to handle the poor. Babylon is saying resources are limited, so hoard what you have, don't give. The Kingdom of God is a system based upon sowing and reaping. You must give in order to receive, and to receive in abundance during this wealth transfer, you will have to be generous to the poor (Proverbs 22:9).

Those who refuse to believe this is true, have never really read the Bible. We talked about Matthew 25 when Jesus will judge us based upon how we treated the suffering and poor among us. Here is another passage that talks about when John the Baptist told people to repent because the Kingdom of Heaven was at hand. He told them to bring forth fruits worthy of repentance (Luke 3:8). In other words, it wasn't good enough just to repent with your heart and your mouth, you had to show evidence of a changed life. The people asked, "What shall we do?" John's answer was not the typical response that would meet the approval of the Babylonian church today. *"He answereth and saith unto them, he that hath two coats, let him impart to him that hath none; and he that hath meat, let him do likewise* (Luke 3:11).*"* In this passage, John the Baptist confirms that God requires that his people to feed and clothe the poor. There is even more. When the tax collectors came and asked John, "What shall we do?" He told them not to cheat anyone, just take what they were owed. The soldiers also asked what they should do and John said, *"Do violence to no man, neither accuse any falsely; and be content with your wages* (Luke 3:12-14).*"*

In the previous chapter we talked about issues of the heart. When it comes to repentance, the heart is where you start. Then, from out of that heart you will produce good deeds worthy of repentance. Babylon would tell you to hoard what you have and cheat if you have to get more. Well, that is how many in the church operate as well. Babylon is not infiltrating the church as some would have you believe. Babylonian thinking is instigated by the church. In fact it started in the church according to the Spirit of God. Our nation is out of order because the church is out of order, and not the other way around. Take Nimrod, who was from the disinherited side of Noah's family. When he could not get the Blessing legitimately, Nimrod declared himself king and took whatever he could from the earth and declared it a Blessing. Nimrod, like Satan exalted his own thrown above God's. It didn't matter what God said, Nimrod was going to rule this world even if he had to go against everything he had known to be true. The Babylonian spirit is a demon with great deceptive powers. Even those who know better could be caught up in the witchcraft that Babylon uses. I wanted to mention this because in our pursuit of God's promise, we will encounter giants and wicked rulers of darkness who will violently come against you. Just like God has a promise for your life. Satan has his demon are poised to keep you from your promise. Remember Satan is a thief. He cannot create an inheritance of his own, so he tries to steal ours. That is what he did to Adam. Because it worked so well, Satan will try it on you too. This is why your heart needs to be fixed on the things of God. This is also why you need to walk in love no matter who comes against you. Keep your eyes on the promise, and let the Holy Spirit fight the enemy for you.

When I went to get my airplane, it should have been a *no brainer*, but then out of nowhere, the enemy attacks me with death threats. I was just obeying God. Why would anyone want to stop me? They were envious and jealous of what God was doing in my life. I was going after the promise God gave me, and they were lusting to take it from me. Some were lusting to destroy the promise before I even got the plane. This is evil that lurks in the hearts of men. These are those who will not obtain anything from God because they are covetous, lusting to have something they are not qualified to receive. *"From whence come wars and fightings among you? Come they not hence, even of your lusts that war in your members? Ye lust, and have not: ye kill, and desire to have, and cannot obtain: ye fight and war, yet ye have not, because ye ask not. Ye ask, and receive not, because ye ask amiss, that ye may consume it upon your lusts (James 4:1-3)."* Babylon entices competition as we said before. She bewitches them into lusting after things, and they really don't know what they are asking for. Babylon likes using things that shine like gold, but it isn't' real gold. When the Lord told me that I had to get married again, prophecy started going forth about the man I would marry. The Lord told me that the devil was going to send all these evil men who would also say I was their wife. He said that these men would be fornicators whose desire would be to kill the dream of God for my life. Ultimately they would kill me. As soon as the prophecies came forth, men were coming out of the woodwork. Every last one opposed the God that was in my life. They were lusting to have me as their wife, but they failed to understand that I was God's daughter and that I was on a path of destiny these men could never handle. One day the Lord showed it to me in the spirit and I laughed out loud at the devil. If any of these men really knew what I was called to do, they would run in the other direction. I have a very dangerous assignment. God gave it to me because the men appointed to this assignment were too fearful to take it on. People have been killed doing what I am doing. To survive this walk, one has to be spiritual mature and very obedient to God. The man **God chose** is already in position. The Lord chose him because he has broad enough shoulders to handle whatever God tells us to do.

Again, Babylon tells you to lust after what looks good. In my case, that is deadly. There were men who tried to hurt me because I did not fit the image they had of me. The Lord explained that they felt entitled to have me as their wife, but when I rejected them, they chose to plot to terrorize and kill me rather than letting me fulfill God's plan for my life. As insane as this sounds, this is the reality of Babylon. Remember, they are under an evil spell because of the evil that is in their hearts. Their lust is insatiable. They are like blood thirsty wolves. The Lord had already told me Satan's plan to use these men to kill me, but that was not to happen. God wanted to warn me of the evil that was plotted against me. Some church leaders have been preaching that the wealth transfer will be easy living from now on. That is not exactly true. You may have more money and possessions than in the past, but you will have even more enemies to deal with. You simply cannot afford to flow with the crowd if you want what God promised. You must be willing to go up against the giants, the evil rulers and terrorists who will be attempting to stop you from reaching your promise. Even while writing this book, I recall that for every promise I had obtained, the enemy came after me with a vengeance. The people he used the most, were those closest to me. They had no idea what they were doing. I simply let them plot and scheme and when I got what the Lord promised, it shut their mouths. The thing they said, I couldn't do, God did for me. The thing they said I could not have or could not afford, the Lord got it for me. Not once did they ask how I was able to do what I do. They just shut up and went about their business. They had to know it was God, but they didn't want to here anything about him, so why bother to share my testimony with them. In the household of faith though, I tell everybody about what the Lord has done. Some of them don't like it either, but when the Lord says tell it, I tell it all and I tell it loud. To God be the glory! This is our fight of faith. We are well able to overcome the giants and terrorists, in order to possess the land (Numbers 13:30).

Now, concerning the Babylonian Church in America, it will fall. Even as the wealth transfer is happening, they will not understand. They have preached against wealth and the Kingdom. They will see it, but they won't experience it (II Kings 7:2). They have been trained by the world to use their human wisdom and reasoning. They behave as though what they see around them is real, and the things of God are imaginary. They have no faith and no power, so when trouble comes, and it will, they will have no defense and no hope. They will hate us even more because we will be thriving in the Kingdom. One reality of the Kingdom is that you cannot receive what you speak against. You shall have what you say, whether negative or positive. Faith speaks (II Corinthians 4:1), and it speaks prophetically with a powerful voice. The devil hates it when faith speaks what God speaks, because he knows that the God kind of faith has the power to change the world in an instant. Now, Babylon will fight to the death to keep her place in this earth, but here is another reality, she cannot win. Her end is coming and coming very soon. God's word will always come to pass. You may speak against it. You can even try to trick God and men, but God's word will come to pass.

The people of God always seem to fight against His Word. God's kids are quite obstinate. We always want to exercise our rights as sons of God without being under the authority of God. We know that we are supposed to be kings and priests (Revelation 1:6), but we fail to realize that God alone can lead the way. We desire to exercise free will in our lives. So does God. That is why he will not force us to obey him. It was never God's desire to be a dictator over the lives of men. God is love (I John 4:8), and we know that love does not seek it's own way (I Corinthians 13:5), but allows others to make their own choices. Loving someone means not forcing your will upon their lives. Loving someone means being wise enough to let them go. If they come back to you freely, then they truly **do** love you. That is how God operates; from the perspective of love. He is a loving Father who wants to share all he has with his kids. God wants us to receive and enjoy our inheritance. That is the **real** reason Jesus came to earth. Jesus even gave us a short cut for successful living on earth. Instead of the Ten Commandments, Jesus gave us only two. For in these two commands all of the law would be fulfilled. Jesus said, *"Thou shalt love the Lord thy God with all thy heart, and with all thy soul, and with all thy mind. This is the first and great commandment. And the second is like unto it, Thou shalt love thy neighbour as thyself. On these two commandments hang all the law and the prophets* (Matthew 22:37-40)." We show our love for God by keeping his commandments, and we demonstrate our love for others by the good deeds of charity.

With God, it's all about relationship. God gave mankind dominion, but he still wants a family relationship with us. Unfortunately, men want free will, but free will is not exactly free as one would expect. With every choice we make, there exists a set of consequences that follow. We cannot escape the consequences for our behaviors. The law of seedtime and harvest will continue as long as the earth remains (Genesis 8:22). Therefore, we will always reap what we have sown. God so graciously sets before us, life and death, blessing and cursing, then he tells us in Deuteronomy 30:19 to chose life. God's plan for us is life and life abundantly (John 10:10). It's the thief that comes to steal, kill and destroy. Babylon is the thief. This is the whole issue surrounding the Tower of Babel. Evil men wanted to steal God's glory for themselves. They chose to depart from their Creator, to exalt themselves above God's throne.

Indeed, humans beings were created in the image and likeness of God, **but** we were never designed to operate above God in this earth. God created all things, and everything he created is being upheld by the word of his power (Hebrews 1:3). All of creation had its beginning and existence with the words which God spoke. Mankind is no different. There exists an illusion that man is created like God, therefore **like** God he can make his own way and succeed. Although God **does** allow men to make a choice whether to follow him or not, but in the end, God's word will have its day. Man will be allowed to rebel, but only a season. Then God will step into that situation, and **His Will**, will be done in the earth. God cannot change his word once it has been spoken in the earth. Humans may arrogantly ignore God and his purpose, but in the end, the word will prevail without fail. Whatever God speaks will accomplish **that** which he has purposed.

I am reminded of the Old Testament story about King Ahab. The Prophet Elijah had spoken a word from God condemning the king to death (I Kings 21:19). Ahab went about his evil ways as if he could outsmart God. So he convinced King Jehoshaphat, to go into battle at Ramothgilead. Ahab enquired of his prophets, but Jehoshaphat asked to enquire of a prophet of the Lord. Ahab didn't like asking God anything because there was one prophet named Micaiah that always spoke against him. Jehoshaphat called Micaiah, and he indeed spoke of the king's defeat if Ahab went to battle. He also spoke evil about his prophets. *"And he said, Hear thou therefore the word of the LORD: I saw the LORD sitting on his throne, and all the host of heaven standing by him on his right hand and on his left. And the LORD said, Who shall persuade Ahab, that he may go up and fall at Ramothgilead? And one said on this manner, and another said on that manner. And there came forth a spirit, and stood before the LORD, and said, I will persuade him. And the LORD said unto him, Wherewith? And he said, I will go forth, and I will be a lying spirit in the mouth of all his prophets. And he said, Thou shalt persuade him, and prevail also: go forth, and do so. Now therefore, behold, the LORD hath put a lying spirit in the mouth of all these thy prophets, and the LORD hath spoken evil concerning thee* (I Kings 22:1-40).*"* Ahab had the Lord's prophet jailed and he went to battle anyway. In an attempt to outsmart God one more time, Ahab wore his armor as a disguise, but he told Jehoshaphat to wear his royal garments to the battle. The Syrian captains were commanded to go after King Ahab. When they saw Jehoshaphat, they began to attack him, thinking that he was King Ahab. Jehoshaphat cried out, and they let him go. In the meantime, a man shoots a random arrow that strikes Ahab between the joints of his armor. The king is fatally wounded. He died that evening in the place and manner in which Elijah had prophesied. The Word of God came to pass even with the Ahab's best efforts to avoid the consequences of his behavior. In the end, God has the last word.

God's word will come to pass no matter what diversionary tactics we humans attempt to avoid the consequences of our sin. In America, God **will** overthrow the Babylonian church in America and scatter his people to the far reaches of the earth preaching the gospel. Sending a great storm against our nation, seems like such a small price to pay in order to bring the lost souls of men into the Kingdom of God. There is the good news, like Jonah, *the word of the Lord* will come to the American Church, the second time (Jonah 3:1), and <u>this time</u>, they **will** obey. The

Christian Church in America almost missed the Kingdom agenda entirely, and the entire Body was in agreement. They thought that Kingdom work was to be done within the confines of the four walls of the church building. The people of God are the church, the *"ecclesia;"* the **elect** who have been called out to represent the Kingdom in this world. God's Kingdom is more than spiritual principles. It's in power and manifestation for all areas of human life. It's a way of loving and sharing with our fellow man, which is not restricted to the church building. It's an ***"Twenty-four seven (24-7), everywhere I go, God goes"*** Kingdom. We don't cease being Americans when we leave one assembly to go to another, neither do the citizens of God's kingdom.

Almighty God will overthrow the Babylonian Church and raise up His Church in this world. Babylon shall fall, just the like Tower of Babel ceased. Nimrod's rule came to an end, and so shall Satan's rule. God **will** restore His Kingdom in this earth, and **it shall** stand forever.

"And in the days of these kings shall the God of heaven set up a kingdom, which shall never be destroyed: and the kingdom shall not be left to other people, but it shall break in pieces and consume all these kingdoms, and it shall stand for ever (Daniel 2:44).*"*

ABOUT THE AUTHOR

Paula Matthews was formally called to the Office of The Prophet in 1997. Shortly thereafter, the Lord said that He was *"sending"* her out like He did the *"first apostles."* Since that time, the Lord has been sending her to strengthen and encourage prophetic leaders who have been embattled by the religious establishment of the Babylonian Church in America.

According to God, many of these *"wounded"* leaders had been *"left on the battle field to die."* Ms. Matthews' assignment was to first, *"heal and deliver"* God's end-time leaders, then *"teach them"* what they needed to know to successfully continue their assignments.

BIBLIOGRAPHY

The Holy Bible: Authorized King James Version. Nashville: Thomas Nelson, 2003.

Copeland, Kenneth; Roberts, Oral; Roberts, Richard. *The Wake-Up Call*. Fort Worth: Kenneth Copeland Publications, 2004.

Matthews, Paula. *The War Journal (1999-2010) Volume I*. Los Angeles: Spirit & Life Publications, 2010.

Josephus, Flavious. *Flavious Josephus: The Complete Works, Translated by William Whiston, NA*.

Matthews, Paula. *The War Journal (1999-2010) Volume II*. Los Angeles: Spirit & Life Publications, 2011.

Matthews, Paula. *American Heritage 101*. Shaker Heights: Spirit & Life Publications[SM], 2012.

Matthews, Paula. EPIC Books And Cafe Presents: *American Heritage Prophecy Series*. Shaker Heights: Spirit & Life Publications[SM], 2013.

Matthews, Paula. *Seeking And Enjoying The True Treasure Of This Life*. Shaker Heights: Spirit & Life Publications[SM], 2013.

Matthews, Paula. *The Glory Revealed Through The Lives Of Ordinary Men*. Shaker Heights: Spirit & Life Publications[SM], 2014.

Matthews, Paula. *Jesus Gave Us Power Over Death*. Shaker Heights: Spirit & Life Publications[SM], 2014.

www.ingramcontent.com/pod-product-compliance
Lightning Source LLC
Chambersburg PA
CBHW060341170426
43202CB00014B/2847